D0645705

YOU BETTER BELIEVE IT

A playboy-turned-Priest
talks to teens

Rev. Kenneth J. Roberts

OUR SUNDAY VISITOR, INC.
PUBLISHER

HUNTINGTON, INDIANA

Nihil Obstat:
Rev. Lawrence Gollner
Censor librorum

Imprimatur:
✠ William E. McManus, D.D.,
Bishop of Fort Wayne-South Bend
February 16, 1977

Acknowledgements: Excerpts from the *New American Bible,* © Confraternity of Christian Doctrine 1970. Excerpts from the English translation·of the Roman Missal, © International Committee on English in the Liturgy, Inc. All rights reserved. Photographs on pp. vi, 29, 34, 60, 94, 98, 108, 161, 179, James J. Dickens; 24, 37, 43, 96, 165, Tom Yahnke, Master Slide, Inc.; 77, 112, 116, 120, Religious News Service; 12, S. K. Dutt, Camera Press, London. Drawing on p. 83 by Sister M. Therese, R.G.S. Painting on p. 87 by Brother Matthew, O.F.F. Cover design by Eric Nesheim.

ISBN: 0-87973-750-6
Library of Congress Catalogue Card Number: 77-84944

PRINTED IN U.S.A.

Our Sunday Visitor, Inc.,
Noll Plaza,
Huntington, Indiana   46750

750

TO ALL THE TEENS
WHO SHARED THEIR QUESTIONS,
DOUBTS, AND FRIENDSHIP,
AND WHO TAUGHT ME TO UNDERSTAND,
THIS BOOK IS WRITTEN
TO TELL THEM THE CHURCH CARES.

I OWE THANKS ALSO TO
THE GOOD SHEPHERD SISTERS
AND THE SISTERS OF THE CROSS
FOR THEIR SUPPORT OF MY WORK.

MAY MARY TAKE
ALL THOSE WHO READ THIS BOOK
AS HER SPECIAL CHILDREN.

K. R.
October 7, 1977
Feast of the Holy Rosary

Preface

What are teenagers saying today? Are they different from young people of other generations? What are their major concerns? Do they believe in God? If so, what are their deepest feelings regarding themselves? Do they have a purpose in life? Do they know why they are here and where they are heading? What are their concepts of Christianity and the person of Christ? Many of them have very negative feelings about the institutional Church, its dogmas, moral teaching and ritual, despite years of Catholic education. Can they be reached? Can they become excited about Jesus but also enthusiastic Catholics? It's not impossible! That's what this book is all about. I believe and know that they *can*.

For the past six years I have been engaged in a full-time retreat apostolate throughout the United States and Canada where I have met with high school and college students, priests, nuns, married couples and singles. I have given days of recollection and evenings of prayer. I have preached parish missions, attended and worked with encounter groups, made a cursillo and prayed with charismatic groups, attended rosary rallies and worked with the media. Yet, nothing has given me more pleasure than our youth.

I believe in our youth and I love them. Perhaps that is the most important requisite for a successful youth apostolate: to love them and have them feel that you love them. It certainly opens the door to dialogue. Without it, that door is closed.

I have written this book in an effort to answer some of the many questions being asked by our young people today. It is, therefore, written in a language which they can relate to and understand.

Since parents, grandparents, aunts, uncles, priests, nuns and teachers also are concerned and care about youth, this book is also for them.

The Church . . . Who Needs It?

I usually don't mind driving long distances. I enjoy the freedom and solitude. But I was uptight during this particular drive from St. Louis to Chicago. It seemed longer than usual. The time was creeping up on me and signs kept flashing SPEED LIMIT . . . 55. I battled to keep from "giving it the gas" as I looked at the long stretch of road before me. There were no cars in sight. It was just the open highway, my radio and me. Each time a sign appeared telling me how many miles to Chicago I was frustrated and panic set in. I looked at my watch, which seemed to shout out, "You're gonna be late . . . you're gonna be late." Then my stomach would growl, "Feed me." The sun was getting hot and I was thirsty and needed to stretch my legs, so I stopped at the next roadside restaurant.

I removed my Roman collar and jacket and threw them on the back seat, then straightened the collar of the sport shirt I was wearing. My mind was preoccupied as I walked toward the wrong door and pushed, almost knocking down a long-haired young man. "Sorry," I apologized as I made room for him to pass.

"It's okay." He smiled as he struggled with the large pack hanging from his shoulder. As he walked away, I noticed a book under his left arm. It looked like a Bible.

A half hour later, I had a full stomach and was more prepared to finish the trip. I had traveled only a few miles when I saw a hitchhiker. It was the young man I had run into at the restaurant and so I pulled over and honked the horn.

"Praise the Lord!" he said as he got in the car. "Thanks for stopping for me."

"How far are you going?" I asked.

"Chicago, but anytime you have to turn off this highway you can just drop me off. The Lord will find another ride for me." He slapped the Bible as if to show his confidence. "Where are *you* heading?"

"Chicago too. Looks like the Lord took real good care of you." We both laughed.

I turned off the radio. "I see you're carrying a Bible."

"Always do now that I'm a Christian. I used to be a Catholic."

I was amused by his emphatic statement. "Don't you feel that Catholics are Christians?"

"Some of them maybe. But the Church confuses the people by throwing in all those rules and ceremonies and junk. All we really need is right in here." He held up the Bible. "We don't need big buildings. We just need to worship God in our hearts. My church is out there." He pointed to the rolling hills. They were spotted with an occasional tree and the scenery was beautiful. "That's how the Lord wanted it. You can see that by reading the New Testament. He always prayed and gave sermons in the countryside. He never planned all those fancy buildings for everyone to gather in and go through the motions of praying."

"Do you feel everything in the New Testament should be taken literally?"

"Of course. That's how the Lord speaks to us."

"And you interpret the Scriptures yourself?"

"Me and the Holy Spirit."

The boy was eager to share what he had found and I had the feeling that he saw a potential convert in me since I showed so much interest in what he was saying. I was curious about him and his philosophy. "You say you used to be a Catholic. Did you go to a Catholic school?"

"Grade school and high school. But I was bored. Mass was always the same old thing. You were never allowed to think for yourself. You never got anything out of it."

"What made you turn to Jesus now?"

"I went to a prayer group one night, but I really went just for laughs — and to see if this one girl was going to be there. But something happened. I really discovered Jesus and the Bible. That's more than the Catholic schools ever did for me."

"You mean they never talked about the Bible and Christ?"

"I guess. They probably tried to, but they were too busy wanting to 'relate.' At least that's what they called it, especially in high school. They told you a bunch of things in grade school and a bunch of new things in high school, and it got me all confused about Christ and the Church. It just didn't turn me on. You don't know how boring it is sitting there at Mass while some priest is mumbling about parish debts or some collection fund. It really turned me off. You've got no idea how boring Mass is."

Trying to suppress my amusement, I asked, "Where do you go to church now?"

"I don't. I don't need to. I read the Bible and it tells me how to live. My church is in my heart. Church people are hypocrites. It's all part of the establishment. You get dressed up on Sunday, sing a few hymns and live like pagans and bitch at each other the rest of the week. They're phony. They don't really know Jesus."

"But now you do?"

"I know Jesus is my Savior. The Church never really showed me that. Too many people love their Church and not Jesus."

"But didn't Jesus found the Church?"

"Not the kind of Churches we have today. 'Denominations are abominations,' and *that's* right from the Scriptures. Right here!" He slapped the Bible for confirmation. "Each Church claims to be Jesus' Church — Catholics, Baptists, Presbyterians, Methodists — and they're all interpreting Scripture their own way."

"But you're saying that the Holy Spirit interprets the Scripture for you. What makes you think you're more right than they are?"

"I just know, that's all. I have the peace of the Lord. In *John*, it says, 'My peace I give to you, my peace I leave to you.' " He began paging through the Bible to find the quotation.

"While you're on *John*, why don't you turn to the sixth chapter. Why don't you read it aloud." I listened to him as he read slowly and reverently, then I stopped him. "Read verse 51 again."

> *I myself am the living bread*
> *Come down from heaven.*
> *If anyone eats this bread, he shall live forever.*
> *The bread I will give is my flesh for*
> *The life of the world. (John 6:51)*

He stopped and looked at me. "So?"

"So where are you going to get that *bread* if you don't go to church?"

"That's all symbolic. He doesn't mean *literally* to eat his body and drink his blood."

"Where does it say that in the Bible? Where does it say that it's only a symbol?"

"It's just common sense."

"I though you were being taught by Scripture, not common sense. Do you believe that God became a man?"

"Sure."

"Common sense didn't teach you that. Why would it teach you that Christ became bread? You're doing the same thing that you claim all denominations are doing, interpreting Scripture in your own way."

The young man's look of self-assurance gave way to a trace of confusion.

"Read further on in *John* and see what Jesus himself said," I suggested.

At this the Jews quarreled among themselves saying "How can he give us his flesh to eat?" Thereupon Jesus said to them:

"Let me solemnly assure you. If you do not eat the flesh of the Son of Man and drink his blood you have no life in you. He who feeds on my flesh and drinks my blood has eternal life, and I will raise him up on the last day. For my flesh is real food and my blood is real drink. The man who feeds on my flesh and drinks my blood remains in me and I in him. Just as the Father who has life sent me and I have life because of the Father, so the man who feeds on me will have life because of me. This is the bread that came down from heaven. Unlike your ancestors who ate and died nonetheless, the man who feeds on this bread shall live forever." After hearing his words, many of his disciples remarked, "This sort of talk is hard to endure. How can anyone take it seriously?" (John 6:52-60)

When he finished he stared at the highway as if he were searching to find the meaning of what he had just read or perhaps trying to think of another argument to present.

"What do you think about that Scripture reading?" I asked.

"I'm still thinking."

"Maybe I can help you. Since you've become quite familiar with the Bible, you know that the Jews already used symbolic bread and wine at Passover. So why wouldn't they be able to accept what Christ had just said to them? They found it hard to endure, but they wouldn't if it had been just a symbol. Why don't you read down to verse 66."

He found the passage and started to read aloud again, but the tone of his voice told me that he was really searching to understand.

From this time on, many of his disciples broke away and would not remain in his company any longer. Jesus said to the twelve, "Do you want to leave me too?" (John 6:66-67)

"My point is, why did Christ let them go if it were only a symbol, or why invite the apostles to do the same? It must have been more than a symbol to him. He didn't call them back. He even risked losing them."

The young man was silent. He obviously needed a chance to roll that last one around a little. Finally he said, "You must be a Catholic. Only Catholics are so hung up about the Body and Blood, Holy Communion and all that. The other Churches think it's a symbol. You're a Catholic, right?"

"Right. But you're wrong about the other Churches. The Eastern Orthodox, the Episcopalians and the Lutherans also believe that Christ meant it literally. They, with six hundred million Roman Catholics, represent 90 per cent of all Christians in the world. But numbers have nothing to do with it. Turn to Paul and see what the early Christians believed. Try First Corinthians 10:16."

He began to read again:

Is not the cup of blessing we bless a sharing in the blood of Christ? And is not the bread we break a sharing in the body of Christ?

"Now try first Corinthians, eleventh chapter, twenty-third to twenty-ninth verse."

"I received from the lord what I handed on to you," he read, *"namely, that the Lord Jesus on the night in which he was betrayed took bread, and after he had given thanks broke it and said, 'This is my body, which is for you. Do this in remembrance of me.' In the same way after supper he took the cup, saying, 'This cup is the new covenant in my blood. Do this whenever you drink it, in remembrance of me.' Every time you eat this bread and drink this cup you proclaim the death of the Lord till he comes! This means that whoever eats the bread or drinks the cup of the Lord unworthily sins against the body and blood of the Lord. A*

man should examine himself first. Only then should he eat of the bread and drink of the cup. He who eats and drinks without recognizing the body eats and drinks a judgment on himself." (1 Corinthians 11:23-29)

"Do you understand it any better now?" I asked.

"I have to think about it."

"Do that, but first read one more quotation. Go to *John*, sixth chapter, fifty-second verse."

"Let me solemnly asure you, if you do not eat the flesh of the Son of Man and drink his blood, you have no life in you." (John 6:52)

After a few minutes of silence the boy frowned at me. "How come you know so much about Scripture?" he asked skeptically. "That's unusual for a Catholic."

"I'm a priest."

"That explains it. You put up pretty good arguments."

"Because I believe in what I'm saying. If I didn't I'd get out. And I wouldn't be racing to get to Chicago now to start another retreat."

"There is one person I learned about while I was Catholic —St. Francis. He didn't need all the big-deal stuff to pray. He found God in nature."

"But he never left the Church to find him. He was still a Catholic and he found Christ in the Mass."

"That was years ago. Priests and nuns are different now."

"Maybe some of them are, but that has nothing to do with the teaching of the Church. The Church still teaches men the same things it taught St. Francis. You don't change the teaching to fit the lives of men, you change the men to obey the teachings. The Catholic Church is not a religious smorgasbord. You can't say, 'I'll take a little of this and a little of that, but I don't like that so I won't take any of it.' With Jesus, it is all or nothing. That's why he gave an ultimatum to the apostles. It isn't enough to say 'I don't like it' or 'I can't understand it' to reject a teaching solemnly taught by Christ. I would love to be free to pick out all the neat and easy ways of following Jesus. I'd love to worship in the woods when I feel like it, but if I am to be a follower of Jesus I must accept *all* he teaches, not just the things that appeal to me. Tell me, where will you go to get his teaching unless you listen to those who are qualified to teach? We need the Church to tell us not just about the Eucharist but about many other things. What is truth? What is sin? To tell us about God, about Christ, about the sacraments and about many moral questions."

During the rest of the drive we had a pleasant exchange of conversation and opinions. Finally, I dropped the boy off at the corner he designated. "Thanks for the ride," he said as he dragged his grip from the car.

"Thank you for the company and conversation. I enjoyed it."

He slammed the door, then peered through the window. "All the things that we talked about—you know, the Church, what it teaches and Christ—well, I'm going to pray and really think about it."

"Pray by all means, but do more than think about it. Because, if what we read in Scripture and what we talked about regarding the teachings of the Church are true, then . . . YOU BETTER BELIEVE IT!"

The Truth, the Whole Truth and Nothing but the Truth

SOUNDS GREAT!
But there are two kinds of truth,
    POSITIVE
        &
    NEGATIVE.
There is a positive truth
In all religions if they worship God
And there is a negative truth also
If they profess to follow their beliefs
But they don't.
Look for the negative truths in the Catholic Church
And you will find them.
Things such as
Corruption and politics among some ecclesiastics,
Too much emphasis on ritual, double standards, lack of strong
    leadership
And many others.
They exist, so they are truths, but NEGATIVE truths.
If one could make a chart with two headings,
POSITIVE TRUTHS and NEGATIVE TRUTHS,
The positive truths would far
Outnumber the negative.

What Is Truth?

There is nothing more awesome than walking into a large assembly hall full of high school students and staring out at hundreds of faces, faces that bear the expression, "Make me listen—I dare you!" After a few deep swallows, I rid myself of the lump in my throat, try to forget that what is in my stomach is trying to leave me, and begin:

"I was a late-comer to the priesthood. I didn't enter the seminary until I was thirty and I wasn't ordained until thirty-five. Why did I become a priest when it seemed I had it made? Why did I give up marriage three weeks before the wedding and vow myself to a life of celibacy?"

I can see by their faces that they are asking the same questions. It is fortunate that I can't hear what answer one of them is whispering under his breath to his smiling companion. But at least they are listening.

I believe that one of the major differences between this age and earlier ones is that this generation seems to have no target for which to aim. "And if you don't have a dream, how you going to have a dream come true?" I believe that if you have no target, you will be nothing and achieve nothing. But if you really believe in something and aim to achieve it, you will find the way to make it work. You must have a target or a dream.

When I was nineteen, I had a dream, an ambition to be rich and see the world. I had a target and wanted to achieve it by the time I was twenty-five. I achieved it one year earlier at twenty-four.

Another major problem is boredom, the most frequent expression we hear today. "It's boring." "I'm bored." I know that feeling only too well. When I achieved my target, at first it was quite exciting traveling around the world. It was great going to nightclubs in Hong Kong, shopping in Tokyo, sightseeing in Rome, getting drunk in Paris, on safaris in Africa. It was fantastic to sunbathe all day at exotic swimming pools and drink all night in jet-set bars. It was thrilling to eat caviar and drink champagne with beautiful blondes, brunettes or redheads. It was all these things for a while. But after five years it was boring!

Where was the excitement in travel when one traveled constantly? Where was the excitement in eating out when one never ate in? Where was the excitement in clothes when you bought new clothes almost daily? I was bored.

When I achieved my original dream of world travel, money, girls and pleasure, I was bored. In my search for a way out all I could see was the negative truth. I saw terrible poverty in Calcutta, the starvation and filth of the multitude and the affluence and plenty of the rich, both in a country where two percent of the population own ninety percent of the wealth, where the rich are really rich and the poor were not just hungry, but starving, dying of hunger in the streets, where the poor had no homes and no food. I looked at the scene, and I saw only the negative truth. I saw SOCIAL INJUSTICE! And so I reached a negative conclusion. How could there be a God? And, if there was a God, he was not just! I had found my excuse. I had found someone to blame. God. It was his world so it was his fault. If he didn't exist, then I had no need to have a conscience. Either way, I had found a way to escape the clutches of the Church and the obligation to obey the commandments.

I easily could have stayed in this negative stage the rest of my life but for a chance encounter with one of the most terrific girls I have ever met. She was a brilliant student who had great beauty and personal wealth. Surely, *she* had everything necessary for personal happiness? Brains, beauty, money—what more could she need?

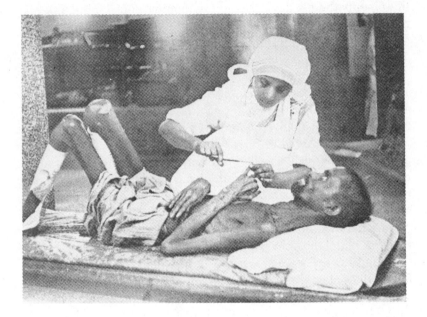

She also came to Calcutta, saw the same filth, the same poverty and the same small minority living in extreme affluence. She also saw the truth of social injustice, but she did not see the negative truth exclusively. She made the right connections with the truth. She could say, "My God, it's *my* fault!" She saw the positive truth also. That is what I see today. Now I know: "If I am not part of the answer, I am part of the problem."

This applies to every problem about which I feel strongly— the generation gap, the credibility gap, the theological gap. You can apply it to problems at school, at home, at church and among your friends. *If you are not part of the answer, you are part of the problem.*

The young lady I described became part of the answer and joined Mother Teresa of Calcutta to work among the poor. She became and is still a nun. When I met her at the convent where she lived among the starving and dying masses in the worst section of the city, I was startled by her amazing beauty. And it was not just physical beauty. I knew many beautiful women in the jet set and among the BOAC girls with whom I flew around the globe. This girl was different. As she stood before me dressed in a white sari bordered with blue and pinned at the neck with a crucifix in the fashion of Mother Teresa's nuns, she was a radiant, vibrant woman with an inner beauty that showed in her eyes and spread in her smile.

I asked her how she could be so happy living in all that filth. Her answer startled me as she again smiled. "How can you be happy living in *your* filth, the filth of your own selfishness. In God's eyes, your life is filthier than this city is to you."

She didn't bring about my instant conversion. I didn't see a blinding light the way St. Paul did or hear voices like St. Joan of Arc, but it was the beginning. Her words stuck. *How could I be happy living in my filth?* Her words remained with me at future cocktail parties. Her face and her happiness were vividly before me each time I saw bathing beauties. *Your life is filthier in the eyes of God than this city is to you. The filth of your own selfishness.* How could I forget that meeting? Her last words to me were, "I will pray for you to become a priest." I smiled. "*Me,* a priest! You had better believe in miracles. I'm engaged to be married. I like life and good living. There is no way I will ever be a priest!"

She didn't answer, only smiled. You see, she did believe in miracles. And that's another point for positive truth. It's only the positive thinkers, who believe in miracles, who have miracles.

Her words didn't convert me or even cause an instant change in my life. They only made me think. How much they made me think!

There is a danger in being bored, for when we are bored we always seek to blame someone or something other than ourselves. We are never the cause of our own boredom—or so we think. It must be someone else. It's their fault or it's because of this or that. This is a danger because bored people are very negative even in their search for truth. Their truth is almost always negative, never positive. It is not enough to have a target, it must be a target and not a maze in which I can get lost. It is not enough to say something is true. Is it *positive* truth?

If you will look at the two diagrams on the next page, you will see what I mean. The top diagram is where I was during my "bored" stage. The bottom diagram shows where I am now. What made the change in what you see? The connecting lines of faith. The black squares are still there, but now they show the white cross.

NEGATIVE TRUTH
FOUR BLACK SQUARES

POSITIVE TRUTH
A WHITE CROSS

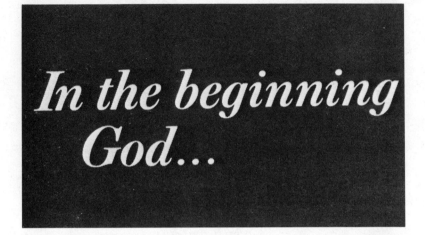

In the beginning God...

How Do We Know There's a God?

I can see the effects of God.
I know there is a wind because
I can see the effects of the wind —
Flags flapping,
Leaves moving,
Your hair becoming ruffled.
I can see what the wind does,
But I can't see the wind.
I can see the effects of God—
All kinds of life,
Nature,
The order of nature,
The vastness of the galaxy.

I can see these things and
They are the effects of God.
But I can't see God.
What kind of energy, mind or intellect conceived
All of these perfect things?
None of them made or conceived themselves.
I can see the presence of a greater power than man.
I call this power GOD.
Atheists claim that energy is responsible for
Creation.
ENERGY must have an intellect to plan a planned creation.
I call this Intellectual Energy GOD.

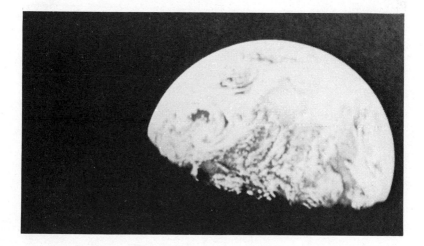

God Is Too Much!!!

God is ETERNAL. God is INFINITE.
NO BEGINNING . . . NO END . . . NO LIMITS . . .
Can you imagine God?
Can you imagine the ocean?
Suppose you had never seen a picture of the ocean.
Suppose it was just a word you had heard
And I was to describe it to you.
The ocean is DEEP and the ocean is SHALLOW.
The ocean is WARM and the ocean is COLD.
The ocean is NOISY and the ocean is QUIET.
The ocean is ROUGH and the ocean is CALM.
Are you getting a picture of the ocean in your mind?
Never. My description is confusing.
You must *experience* the ocean in order to know it.
Suppose I took some water from the ocean
And put it in a bottle.
"LOOK! HERE IS THE OCEAN!"
Can you see its depth?
Can you feel the salty water around you?
Can you hear the noise of the waves?
Can you see its
Power?
Beauty?
Vastness?

Can you experience all these things by looking
At this bottle of ocean water?
If I poured it on you you would learn one thing,
Its *wetness*.
Now you know just a little about the ocean.
If I took you to a swimming pool, you could experience
More of the ocean.
If I took you to a lake, you could experience even more.
Abraham takes us to the pool.
Moses takes us to the lake.
Jesus takes us to the ocean.
The Holy Spirit pulls us into the ocean.
We can experience it.
Even if I am in the ocean, I can only know that
Part where I am.
My part of the ocean can be warm,
Your part can be cold.
Where I am, it could be shallow.
Where you are, it could be deep.
Where I am, it could be calm.
Where you are, it could be rough.
If these things are true of the ocean,
How much truer are they of an infinite God?
Everyone has a different idea of God.
He's *big, everywhere, all-knowing, all-wise, all-loving*.
We get a little better idea of God
Through love.

God is love.

God is good.

God is kind.

God is merciful.

And God loves me.

"I Don't Know How to Love Him"

It's hard to love an intellectual energy,
So God sent Jesus to show us how to love him.
Jesus says,
"When you pray, say *Our Father.*"
Think of a father-child relationship.
Some teenagers may think of their fathers and think of
      A father who is always shouting,
      A father who is always drunk,
      A father who beats you up,
      A father who never listens.
That's a bad picture of a father.
Apply that picture to God:
      God the shouter,
      God the drunk,
      God the beater,
      God who never listens.
Now picture a good father:
      Somebody who provides life for you,
      Somebody who cares about you,
      Somebody who is there when you need him,
      Somebody who listens and always understands,
      Somebody who loves you.
That's the kind of father GOD is.

"How Come God Put Such a Mess in the World?"

Poor God.
When things go wrong, we always blame him.
People kill each other,
Blame God.
People starve,
Blame God.
People hurt each other,
Blame God.
But God didn't want it that way.
He gave us commandments to live by
And free will to choose to obey his commandments
Or reject them.
If we all obeyed God's laws
There would be
     Love
     Equality
     Peace
     A perfect world.
We have something no other living creature has,
A free will.
We are free to choose God and his laws or reject them.
And even when we disobey
He doesn't give up on us.
He takes us back.

"Why Was I Born?"

Why did God make us?
God made us to KNOW HIM
    to LOVE HIM
    to SERVE HIM
In this world and be happy with him
Forever in the next.
We use these words many times about God
And don't realize it.
Think of the song "Day by Day":

> *Day by day, day by day,*
> *Oh, dear Lord,*
> *Three things I pray,*
> *To see you more clearly* (KNOW HIM)
> *To love you more dearly* (LOVE HIM)
> *To follow you more nearly* (SERVE HIM)
> *Day by day.*

You kids are saying it all the time,
Just using different words.
If you live these words
You have all of eternity to be happy.
The next time you hear the song,
LISTEN . . . REMEMBER.
God made me to KNOW him, to LOVE him, to SERVE him
And be happy with him for eternity.
That eternity is a fantastic selling point
For living those words.

"Sometimes, I Don't Like Me!"

That feeling is not unusual when in your teens.
You're between childhood and adulthood.
There are feelings of
Insecurity,
Inferiority,
Self-consciousness
During these changing years.
Teens cover up these feelings by
Flocking together,
Dressing alike,
Talking alike
And rebelling alike.
They want to *fit in the crowd.*
So, sometimes, they act
Conceited, indifferent, rebellious
And knock the establishment.
They try to act as if
They've got it all together
But often only act like a
Smartass.
In a crowd, they feel at home.
There is strength in numbers.
But when you are alone
Where is your strength?
Can you stand silence?
Do you like to be alone with your thoughts?
What are your thoughts?
Why do you need constant action?
To drown your thoughts, maybe?
Do you really want to think
About *you?*

When I ask a group of kids to
Be quiet for a minute of silent prayer,
Freshmen and sophomores
Sometimes giggle.
Silence makes them uncomfortable.
It's not abnormal to feel uncomfortable
At this age.
You are becoming *you.*
It takes time.
You don't become tall
By wishing.
You don't grow overnight in size.
Why should you grow emotionally overnight?
You must live,
Experience,
Feel.
Time is required to mature.
Relax.

Seek the Lord while he may be found,
    call him while he is near.
Let the scoundrel forsake his way,
    and the wicked man his thoughts;
Let him turn to the Lord for mercy;
    to our God, who is generous in forgiving.
For my thoughts are not your thoughts,
    nor are your ways my ways, says the Lord.
As high as the heavens are above the earth,
    so high are my ways above your ways
    and my thoughts above your thoughts.

Isaiah 55.6-9

Junk

Charlie was a drunk. He beat his wife. And he didn't
    like himself.
He would say:
    I'm no good.
    I'm rotten.
    I'm useless.
    I'm garbage.
But Charlie was a good artist.
"I'm proud of my work," he would say.
I asked him, "What would you do if I
Told you that your paintings were junk?"
He got angry.
"I'd belt you in the mouth."
But Charlie keeps telling God,
"Hey God, you made *junk* when you made me!"
That's what you kids do when you
Put yourselves down.
Quit knocking God's work.
He made you.
And God doesn't make junk!

33

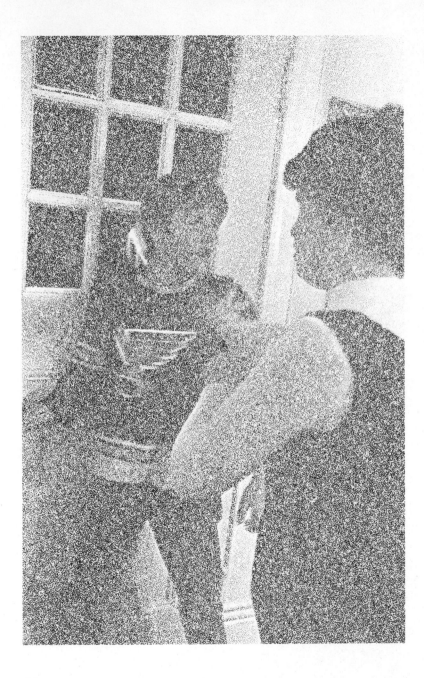

"Parents Don't Understand Us!"

Whose fault is that?
Sometimes parents expect too much.
They want kids to act like adults.
They forget that
Once they too were teenagers.
> They showed off.
> They rebelled.
> They questioned.
> They did "their own thing."

EXPERIENCE
&
RESPONSIBILITY
Made them adults.
AND TIME.

Ask them how they felt when they were
Your age.
They love to reminisce.
Then think about this:
Seeds are not flowers,
But seeds *become* flowers,
Then *they* have seeds.
God knows your real value
And he knows your potential.
Believe in yourself and maybe others will
Believe in you too.
What you *are* is God's gift to you.
What you *become* is your gift to God.
He understands.

Somebody Loves You

Sandy was only thirteen, but already she wanted to "end it all." She wanted to die. The court had assigned her to an institution run by nuns who specialize in problem teenagers. She refused to speak, eat or communicate in any way. I met her after she had been there for three weeks. She was sitting in a large room crying, her hands covering her face.

The sisters were concerned for her health and so it had been arranged for her to be transferred to a psychiatric hospital the next day. As I passed her I put my arm around her, hoping to comfort her, but she reacted violently by kicking, biting and clawing at me. I was frustrated in my attempts to help her but, quite by accident, I discovered a way to help many.

I noticed that she kept her face covered. I still had not seen it. As I was leaving I remarked, "I will never know whether you are pretty or not because you won't let me see your face." I don't know what happened inside her head, but I do know that she wanted to know if someone thought she was pretty or not, for she lowered her arm and exposed a very sad, tearstained face. "You really are pretty," I told her.

She forced her face into a big smile and I discovered that day that it is impossible to smile and remain angry or depressed, for if you hold on to your anger, bitterness or depression you can only sneer. To really smile, you have to let go of the bad feelings. That's what happened to Sandy when she smiled. At least for the moment, she forgot her problems.

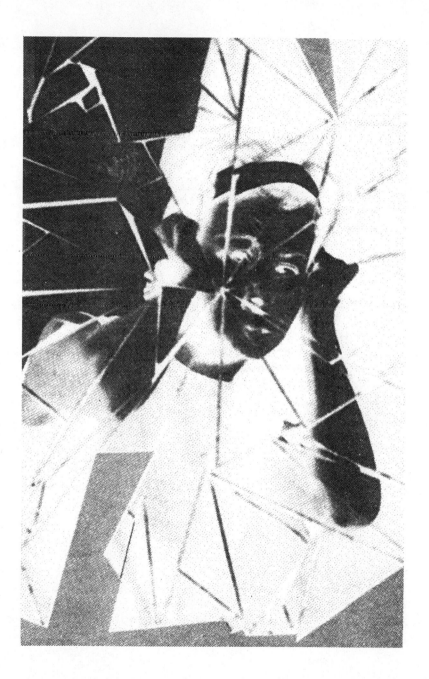

"You really are beautiful," I said. That did the trick. She took my hand and asked, "Do you want to see my room?"

Once in her room, she went to a drawer and showed me all of her cherished belongings which were wrapped up in an old Christmas box. There were photos, pressed leaves and scraps of paper with her personal jottings. One that really caught my eye was written in black crayon and huge lettering. It read:

> My name is Sandy and I loved my Mama and my Mama loved me, but my Mama died February 21. I loved my Papa too but he left home when Mama went blind. I loved my brothers but they did bad things to me and they went away too.

Each of the following lines told of another misery, another hurt, of more depression that she had experienced until finally at the end she wrote:

I wonder why God made me. I wish I were dead.

"Don't you know why God made you, Sandy?" I asked, feeling her hurt and confusion.

"No." She didn't know and she said, "I don't care." But she did care or she would never have asked that question, not even in her private diary.

"You really loved your mother, right?"

"Yes, and she loved me too."

"Supposing your mother could pick any girl in the whole universe, whom would she have picked." I waited for her reply as she thought about it. Any other child would have immediately responded, "Me!" But Sandy wasn't just any girl. She had been deeply hurt emotionally. Sandy answered my question with the hesitancy of someone who is answering an oral examination and who is not certain of the answer to the question asked. She said, "Me?" with a question mark. She wasn't even certain of her own mother's love. She said her mother loved her, but she didn't feel it deep down. Many of us say, "God loves me," but we don't feel it deep down either.

I don't know who Sandy's mother would have picked, but I do know who God picked. God made Sandy and God made each one of us for the same reason.

God needs Sandy.

God needs you.

God needs me.

Not a need as I need food to live but a need as I need this chair in which I am sitting.

I chose that need.

God chose his need in you

And God doesn't make anything he doesn't need.

In all the universe

There is only one YOU.

You are as unique as the sun.

There has never been another you.

There will never be another you.

God needs *you*—

In sadness.

In joy.

In peace.

In pain.

He chose you to love with

The kind of love that only

You can give him.

Once you realize God's love for you

And your love for him

No one can take it from you, not even death.

I told Sandy that although she had kept her face hidden and nobody could tell if she were pretty or not, God had known how pretty she was all along. And he loved her. He needed her to love him back in the only way she could. "God believes in you, Sandy." And she began to believe in herself. Now she could love herself and love her neighbor too.

Three years later, I saw Sandy again, a fine young Christian who is now helping others to believe in themselves.

"Everybody's Talking
At Me"

So you get confused about YOU.
And like all teenagers, and adults too,
You want to be understood.
Don't be uptight.
God knows YOU.
He picked YOU to be YOU
And he will never
Turn away from YOU.
Don't turn away from HIM.

Speak to God

Oh Lord, you have probed me and you know me.
You know when I sit and when I stand.
You understand my thoughts from afar.
My journeys and my rest you scrutinize.
With all my ways you are familiar.
Behold, oh Lord, you know the whole of it.
Behind me and before, you hem me in
And rest your hand upon me.
Such knowledge is too wonderful for me,
Too lofty for me to attain.
Where can I go from your spirit?
From your presence, where can I flee?
If I go up to the heavens you are there.
If I sink to the nether world you are present there.
If I take the wings of dawn,
If I settle in the farthest limits of the sea,
Even there your hand shall guide me
And your right hand hold me fast.
If I say surely the darkness shall hide me
And the night shall be my light—
For you darkness itself is not dark
And the night shines as the day.
Darkness and light are the same.
Truly you have formed my inmost being.
You knit me in my mother's womb.
I give you thanks that I am fearfully, wonderfully made.

Wonderful are your works.
My soul you also knew full well.
Nor was my frame unknown to you
When I was made in secret,
When I was fashioned in the depths of the earth.
Your eyes have seen my actions.
In your book they are all written.
My days were limited before one of them existed.
How weighty are your designs, O God,
How vast the sum of them.
Were I to recount them they would outnumber the sands.
Did I reach the end of them
I should still be with you. (Psalm 139:1-18)

"What's All This Stuff About Sin?"

SIN is a word nobody wants to use these days.
Sin is evil.
Sin is contrary to God's law.
Sin is an absence of a necessary good.
But sin does exist.
We sin when we choose not
To follow God's plan.
Rather than say that we have sinned,
It is easier to say that we are not
Choosing evil, that we are choosing
Good.

>Hitler did it.
He didn't kill Jews and call it a sin—
But it *was* murder.
Hitler called it "liberating Germany."
Russia marched into Hungary not to conquer
Hungary, but to
Liberate it.

>>Women don't say that they are
Murdering babies
When they have an abortion.
They say that they
Are *liberating* women.

>>>Teens don't call premarital sex
Sins against purity.
They call it
"Freedom of expression."

Is the Church

Still Hung Up

on Sex?

The Church isn't hung up on sex at all,
But some individuals are.
The Church still holds fast to the
Sixth and ninth commandments:

Thou shalt not commit adultery.

Thou shalt not covet thy neighbor's wife.

Teens say,
"That's for married people,
Not for us!
We're not married."
St. Paul says, "No fornicators shall
Enter Heaven."
That means any single people who are
Having sexual activity.
So take the blinders off!
Forget that "in" philosophy,
"If it feels good, do it."
No matter how you cut it,
You're breaking one of God's commandments.
And contrary to what some people
Think, the Church thinks that
SEX IS BEAUTIFUL.
Sex is God's most beautiful gift.
For a man to love a woman
And be joined to her
And she to him
And both in God—
That's beautiful.

Sex, to be as God planned it,
Must be like God himself,
THREE IN ONE.
For the sexual act to be truly beautiful
In all its perfection
It must be a TRIANGLE.

If one of these angles
Is missing,
There is an absence of a
Necessary good. There is
SIN.

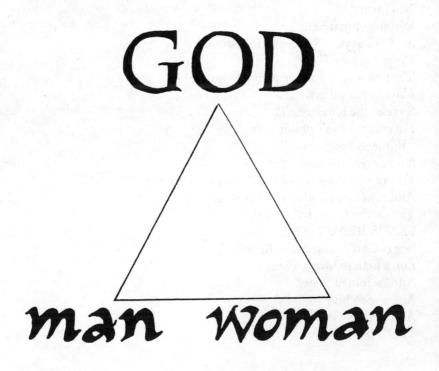

"Everybody's Doing It!"

It's a cop-out
To say
"Everybody is doing it."
It doesn't make it right.
And even if they were doing it,
Which they are not, it
Still doesn't make it right.
In actual fact, surveys record
That one-third of the kids *are* doing it
And another third are *saying*
That they are doing it.
Anyone who tells you
Sex is okay, "Enjoy it,"
Is not teaching what is in
Conformity with the Church.
Teaching sex is okay.
And you can 'Enjoy it' after marriage.
If you feel pressured into
Taking part in sexual activity
To be part of the crowd,
You're falling into the trap.
You excuse it with
"Everybody is doing it."

Take the blinders off.
You have a lax conscience.

"If the Church Says Sex Is Good, How Come Priests & Religious Aren't Married?"

Priests and religious make
The ultimate sacrifice by
Staying single.
To be married would require
Them to give themselves to their families.
By remaining single, they are free
To give themselves, their time,
Their work,
Their love,
Their service,
To those in need.
Today there is an added benefit
To the celibate life.
It is living witness
To self-control
In a world where so
Much emphasis is put on sex.
Many argue that other religions
Do not require such sacrifices from
Their clergy, and that is fine.
But the Church has the right
To specify certain requirements

For those who wish to serve God
And the Church in a special way.
Just as an employer has the right
To stipulate certain requirements
For his employees.
You see it in the want ads
All the time:
"Only college graduates need apply."
The Church specifies its requirements:
Physically healthy,
Of good moral character,
Average intelligence
And single.
The fact that other religions do not
Require the same qualifications has
Nothing to do with us.
Some people say,
"Celibacy is unnatural."
I agree with that.
Celibacy *is* unnatural.
Celibacy is *super*natural.
For, without God's help,
We couldn't do it.
Some men and women cannot live
A celibate life so they choose marriage.
This is what Christ says:

His disciples said to him,
"If that is the case between man and wife,
it is better not to marry."
Jesus said,
"Not everyone can accept this teaching,
only those to whom it is given to do so.
Some men are incapable
of sexual activity from birth,
some have been deliberately made so,
and some there are
who have freely denounced sex
for the sake of God's reign.
Let him accept this teaching who can."

Matthew 19.10-12

"The Church Says NO to Everything!"

Not true.
There are ten commandments
Which we share with the Protestants and the Jews.
The first three are
"Thou shall's."
They tell us how we should act
Toward God.
The other seven tell us how
We should act toward our fellow man.
One commandment that is another
"Thou shall" is the fourth,
Honor thy father and mother.
Don't overlook that one.
With all the talk about the
Generation gap,
Teens excuse their rudeness by saying
"They don't understand me."
That's no excuse for disobedience.
And don't kid yourself.
Fornication isn't the only sin.
How honest are you?
Did you ever steal?
What about jealousy?
Let's go through those ten commandments again.
And in good conscience.

You can only have a well-informed conscience
If you know *what God has commanded.*
We should always follow a
Well-informed conscience.
A lax conscience
Is like an unused muscle.
It's there, but it
Isn't functioning properly.
A person with a lax conscience
Chooses sin but makes it appear good.
He says
"Everybody is doing it,
It must be okay.
If it feels good, do it."

God wouldn't have given us sex
If we were not meant to enjoy it.
God gave us food to enjoy, too,
But not so we can gorge ourselves and
Become sick.
Sex is intended for marriage.
No fornicator can enter heaven.
Sex is one of God's beautiful gifts,
But it is marked like a Christmas package:
DO NOT OPEN TILL CHRISTMAS . . .
DO NOT USE UNTIL AFTER MARRIAGE.

Not all sins are those we
Deliberately *do*.
What about all the times we
Have the power to make things right
But don't?
How many times do we refuse to extend
A kindness because others will think
That we aren't "with it"?

The

Ten Commandments

Are Still Around?

1. *I am the Lord, your God, you shall not have strange gods before me.* (And that means putting too much emphasis on material things too.)

2. *You shall not use God's name in vain.* (How often do you say without thinking, "For God's sake" or "O, my God"?)

3. *Keep holy the sabbath day.* (How often do you miss Sunday Mass?)

4. *Honor your father and mother.* (Do you always obey your parents?)

5. *You shall not kill.* (But do you ever fight and argue in order deliberately to hurt someone?)

6. *You shall not commit adultery.* (What about premarital sex? Dirty movies? Pornography?)

7. *You shall not steal.* (Did you ever just pick up a small item from the store?)

8. *You shall not lie.* (What about the excuses you dream up when backed into a corner?)

9. *You shall not covet your neighbor's wife.* (Do you ever entertain impure thoughts about someone?)

10. *You shall not covet your neighbor's goods.* (Are you jealous because someone has more going for him than you?)

Teenagers Are the Bad Guys!

Not at all.
Adults are guilty of
Choosing a sin and making
It appear as a good.
Everybody likes to talk about
Others' sins, never his own.
Women will complain about how
Kids carry on:
"All that sex,"
"All that dope,"
"All that vandalism."
"They are destroying all that is good!"
They will shout.
But ask them about gossip
And they say,
"Oh, that's not a sin!"
But aren't they *hurting* others?
Their reputation?
Their good name?
And men complain about kids stealing.
But how many pad their expense accounts?
Take off a few hours early while on company time?
Cheat on their income tax?
Kids aren't the bad guys!
Anyone who falls into the category of
Not obeying God's commandments
Is just as guilty as the teenager.
When we sin, we're *all* bad guys,
But God always takes us back.

God Speaks to You

Can you not realize that the unholy will not fall heir to the Kingdom of God? Do not deceive yourselves: no fornicators, idolaters, or adulterers, no sodomites, thieves, misers, or drunkards, no slanderers, or robbers will inherit God's Kingdom. And such were some of you. But you have been washed, consecrated, justified in the name of our Lord Jesus Christ and in the Spirit of God. "Everything is lawful for me." . . . But that does not mean that everything is good for me. "Everything is lawful for me." But I will not let myself be enslaved by anything. "Food is for the stomach and the stomach for food, and God will do away with them both in the end." But the body is not for immorality: it is for the Lord, and the Lord is for the body. God, who raised up the Lord, will raise us also by his power.

Do you not see that your bodies are members of Christ? Would you have me take Christ's members and make them the members of a prostitute? God forbid! Can you not see that the man who is joined to a prostitute becomes one body with her? Scripture says, "The two shall become one flesh." But whoever is joined to the Lord becomes one spirit with him. Shun lewd conduct. Every other sin a man commits is outside his body. But the fornicator sins against his own body. You must know that your body is a temple of the Holy Spirit, who is within, the spirit you have received from God. You are not your own. You have been purchased, and at a price! So glorify God in your body.

(I Corinthians 6:9-20)

"What Is a Christian?"

From New York
to San Francisco,
I have asked kids one question
and I have never received
the complete answer.
See how you score.

If you answer
*It doesn't make any difference what religion you are as long as
you are good.*
>   You would be wrong.
*A Christian is someone who treats others the way he wants to be
treated.*
>   Wrong again.
Someone who believes in Jesus Christ.
>   Incomplete.
*A Christian is someone who is always doing nice things for peo-
ple.*
>   Not quite.
A Christian is someone who goes to church and leads a good life.
>   Better—but still not the full answer.
A Christian believes in God.
>   So do the Jews, Hindus and Buddhists.
A good person is Christian.
What about the Jews, the Buddhists and Hindus?
Are't *they* good people?
Somehow the words
"Good" and "Christian"
Have become synonymous.
But to say,
"A good person is a Christian"
Doesn't tell you what
A Christian really is.

Jews are good.
Hindus are good.
Buddhists are good.
Substitute for the word "Christian"
And say
A good person is a Jew.
That doesn't tell us
What a Jew believes.

This is the definition of a Christian:

SOMEONE WHO IS BAPTIZED
AND BELIEVES IN
JESUS CHRIST AS GOD AND MAN.
HE SUFFERED AND DIED
FOR ALL MEN
AND ROSE FROM THE DEAD.

Let's take each part separately.

SOMEONE WHO IS BAPTIZED . . .
"Unless you be born again of water,
you cannot enter the kingdom of heaven."

. . . BELIEVES IN JESUS CHRIST AS GOD AND MAN . . .
Jesus, the second person of the Trinity,
took on a human nature.
He was God.
He was a real man.
He felt everthing a man could feel.

. . . HE SUFFERED . . .
He felt the nails in his hands and feet.
He felt the spear.
He cried out because of the pain.

. . . HE DIED FOR ALL MEN . . .
He was crucified and hung on the cross
until he took his last breath.
He died for *all* men,
whether they be black, white, yellow, or red.

. . . HE ROSE FROM THE DEAD.
The tomb was empty.
He appeared to his disciples,
who preached,
He whom you crucified has risen. Alleluia.

"How Do I Know Jesus Was God?"

THE RESURRECTION!

Without it Jesus would be
Just another man.
Other men were miracle workers,
Worked miracles with God's power.
The only miracle that is unique
To Jesus
Is the Resurrection.
No ordinary man can rise from the dead.
The empty tomb must be accepted
Or rejected.
If the tomb were not empty,
Why didn't someone produce the body?
It would be stupid to say that
Nobody was curious enough to go
Check for themselves.
They knew where he was buried.
Surely, the Jewish priests would be
Anxious to stop this rumor.
Surely, Pontius Pilate would
Be interested enough to face the people
to show them the *dead* Jesus
If the tomb wasn't empty and
The body was there?

The Body Was Stolen!

Who took it?
His enemies?
For what reason?
To prove He was God?
I hardly think so.
What about his friends, the disciples?
If they had the body,
They would have proof that
Jesus wasn't God.
And all the apostles,
With the exception of John,
Died a martyr's death
While still proclaiming
Jesus as the Lord.
Why would they die for a lie?

Crazy Christians
Who Hallucinate . . .?

The Apostles Were Crazy.

Were they?
They claimed to have seen the Lord.
Perhaps their guilt caused them
To imagine it?
Mary Magdalene loved him.
Did she *imagine* it was Jesus she saw?
What about Thomas, the doubter?
Did he become a part of this mass
Hysteria?
He had to have it proved to him
And he died because of his belief.
What about Saul, the bigot?
He hated and persecuted Christians.
What did it take to convert him?
What would it take to convert
Mao Tse-tung or Madalyn Murray O'Hair
To Christianity?

A bigot has a closed mind.
Can you, by mere reason and argument,
Convert a bigoted Democrat
To Nixon—or
A bigoted Republican
To Carter?
What would it take to

Convert a bigoted racist
To integration?
What would it take to convert
A bigoted religious fanatic to
Love his enemy?
A MIRACLE!

Saul, the bigoted racist,
The religious fanatic,
Is converted and speaks
Of his encounter with the Lord. There is
A blinding flash and a voice:

> *"Saul, Saul, why do you persecute me?"*
> *"Who are you, Lord?"*
> *"I am Jesus whom you persecuted."*

If that miracle had never occurred,
How would we account for Saul's conversion?
Paul, the apostle of the Gentiles
Who had his head chopped off,
FOR JESUS, HIS LORD.

God speaks to you through Jewish prophets.

> *But you, Bethlehem-Ephrathah*
> *Too small to be among the clans of Judah*
> *From you shall come forth for me*
> *One who is to be ruler in Israel;*
> *Whose origin is from of old from*
> *Ancient Times. (Micah 5:1)*

Prophetic for God to be born in Bethlehem as a man? Didn't these words come true in Jesus?

> *He shall stand firm and shepherd his flock*
> *In the majestic name of the Lord God*
> *And they shall remain, for now his greatness*
> *Shall reach the ends of the earth. He shall be*
> *Peace. (Micah 5:3)*

Prophetic for Jesus, the Good Shepherd whose kingdom is world-wide? Didn't these words come true in Jesus?

> *The Virgin shall be with child and bear a son and shall name Him Immanuel. (Isaiah 7:14)*

Immanuel means "God with us." Prophetic? Didn't these words come true in Mary and Jesus? Prophetic?

> *For a child is born to us, a son is given us.*
> *Upon his shoulders dominion rests. They name*
> *Him wonder, counselor, God-hero,*
> *Father-Forever, Prince of Peace. (Isaiah 9:5)*

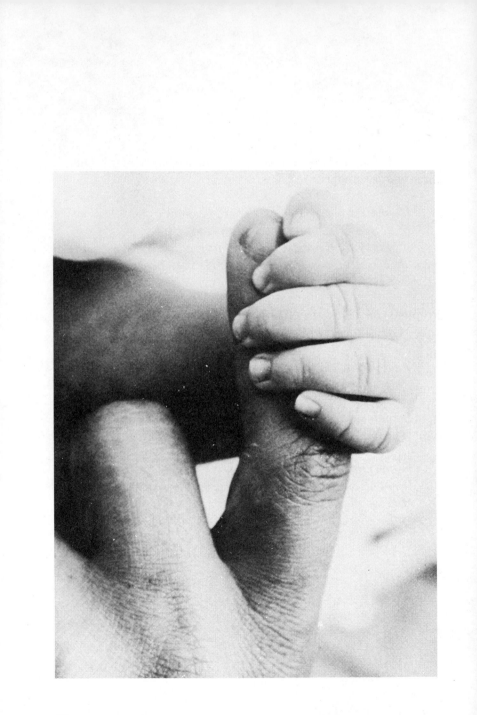

Jesus Christ,
a Real Superstar?

Jesus was a real baby,

And, if he had been in a room
Filled with other babies,
No one would have picked him out as
The Son of God.
He wet his diaper.
He cried when he was hungry.
He crawled on his tummy.
He tried to walk and
Probably stumbled and fell.
The baby Jesus didn't sit
On a little throne and with
A little pink hand give
His blessings.
He lay in his crib and
Reached for his toes,
Played with his fingers
And probably cried when
He got bored and wanted
His mother to pick him
Up and rock him for a while.
Jesus was a real baby.

Jesus was a real boy.

He played with the other
Kids in the village.

He got dirty.
He climbed trees,
He went fishing.
He was called from play
To have dinner with Mary and Joseph.
Kids stood outside his door and shouted,
"Hey Jesus, can you come out to play?"

He helped his mother with the heavy chores.
He and Joseph made chairs,
Maybe even toys,
A sling shot,
A bow and arrows.
And he probably thought his dad
Was the best dad in town,
Something many of us forget about—
Joseph. He must have been pretty
Special.
He was the man
Whom Christ could use as an
Example of what a man should be.

Jesus was a real teenager,

And he felt the generation gap too.
What about when he took off
On his own and wandered
Into the temple?
His parents were looking for him
For three days but
He was busy
"Doing his thing."
When they found him,
What did he say?
"Why did you look for me?"
In his youth, he perhaps

Didn't realize how much his parents
Were worried.
He was probably restless
Like most teenagers,
But he was obedient.
He went home with them
"And was subject to them."
In other words,
He did as he was told
Because he loved them.
But he may have doubted their
Rules and regulations for him
At times, because
Jesus was a real teenager.

Jesus was a real man.

Maybe tall, about six feet,
Probably had strong arms
And a muscular frame from
Working as a carpenter.
May have had calluses on his
Hands too.
But he must have been
Quite a figure walking
Through the streets,
Holding the attention of
Everyone who saw him.
He wasn't worried about
Gossip because out of
Love and compassion, he
Befriended a prostitute, Mary Magdalene.
And he wasn't a snob.
He didn't choose his followers
Because they were intellectual.
He chose simple men, fishermen.

He must have had a powerful voice
To preach along the countryside
And capture everyone's attention.
He was considerate, for he was
Aware of people's needs.
Remember the loaves and the fishes?

Christ must have loved children,
For even when he stopped to rest
And the children ran to him
He told the apostles to
Leave them alone.
"Suffer the little children to
Come unto me."
They must have pulled on his beard,
Bounced on his knee,
Hugged him,
Asked him to play with them.
And he probably did.

And I'll bet Jesus laughed a lot too.
Peter was always doing something
Impetuous.
He probably made the apostles
Laugh when he felt they needed
A rest and some recreation.

He was compassionate.
He felt the suffering of others.
He cured the sick,
The blind,
The lame.
He must have had eyes that seemed
To look into your very soul.

And he had a temper.
Remember the merchants at the temple.

He turned their tables over.

Jesus was a real man.
Jesus had friends,
Special friends,
Just like you and me.
Out of all the thousands of
People he met,
He chose only twelve.
And from those twelve, he chose
Only three
To go to the mountain
And witness his Transfiguration.
Only Peter, James and John
Saw the Divine light
That shone through
Jesus' humanity.
Only Peter, James and John
Were invited to the garden
To watch Jesus in his agony
And his fear.
But John was his closest friend,
His best friend.
Of all the disciples that Jesus loved,
John alone was at the foot of the cross.
In his humanity, Jesus wanted to
Share everything with his close friends
Just as we want to share our feelings
With our close friends.
Jesus had friends and
He was a friend.
And Jesus *is* a friend.

"Who Cares?"

Jesus knelt in the garden,
Worried,
Ill.
WHO CARES?
Jesus was
Depressed.
He trembled.
WHO CARES?
Jesus asked,
"Will you not watch one
Hour with me?"
They were sleeping.
WHO CARES?
Jesus was sad,
Alone,
He sweat blood.
WHO CARES?
Jesus cried,
"Father, if it be possible,
Let this chalice pass from me!"
WHO CARES?
"Not my will but thine be done!"
WHO CARES?
Judas kisses him.
He betrays him.
WHO CARES?

SISTER M. THERESE R.S.

83

Pilate questions him.
Herod mocks him.
WHO CARES?
Jesus is beaten,
Crowned with thorns.
The mob is wild.
WHO CARES?
"We have no king
But Caesar.
Crucify him, Crucify him!"
WHO CARES?
Jesus drags the heavy cross
To Calvary.
He stumbles and falls.
Oh, how it hurts!
WHO CARES?
Blood streams down his back.
His body is torn with pain.
Through bloodstained eyes
He strains to see.
WHO CARES?
His mother follows,
Weeping helplessly.
That's my son!
WHO CARES?
Jesus falls again.
The mob screams.
They kick and punch him.
WHO CARES?
Perverts laugh as
He stands naked before them.
He stretches out his arms
Upon the cross to be nailed.
THUMP, THUMP, THUMP, THUMP.
What pain!
WHO CARES?

Blood runs down in drops
Upon the ground.
O God, it hurts!
WHO CARES?
A few women and John
Stand at the cross.
Where are all the others?
Is this all that's left of them?
WHO CARES?
Jesus hangs on the cross.
It's hard to breathe.
He gasps for breath.
His throat is dry.
WHO CARES?
Oh, the pain, the pain!
His arms, his legs.
He can't breathe.
He chokes out his last words.
"Mother, there is your son."
"I'm thirsty."
"My God, my God, why have you forgotten me?"
The crowd laughs.
WHO CARES?
"It is finished."
WHO CARES?

Mary holds the dead Jesus
In her outstretched arms.
She thinks back to Bethlehem
When a small baby rested there.
This is the same small child
To whom she gave birth, whom she laid in a manger,
The same baby who learned to talk.
This was her body, her blood.
She thinks back to Nazareth
And the happy times,

Times when Jesus made her laugh,
Times when she proudly watched
Him grow and climb on Joseph's knee,
Times when, even more proudly, she
Listened from the crowd to
Her Son, the Messiah, the King,
Times when she entertained his friends,
When she cooked for him his favorite foods
Or merely watched him sleep
When no one else was there,
Times that just the two of them shared.
She looked down upon her dead son in her arms
And cried,
They have killed my son. . . .
Is that all there is?

Why
Don't the Jews
Accept Jesus
as the Messiah?

The Jews are still waiting
for the Messiah
to come.
Yet, in the Old Testament,
the Jewish Bible,
we read a precise description
of Jesus Christ,
his passion and death.

God Speaks through His Prophets
in the Old Testament

Spurned and we held him in no esteem (they mocked him).
Yet it was our infirmities that he bore,
Our sufferings that he endured,
While we thought of him as stricken,
As one smitten by God and afflicted.
But he was pierced (the nails pierced his hands and feet)
For our offenses,
Crushed for our sins (he fell under the weight of the cross).
Upon him was the chastisement (he carried the cross)
That makes us whole.
By his stripes (the scars of the scourging)
We were healed.
We had all gone astray like sheep,
Each following his own way.
But the Lord laid upon him
The guilt of us all (he took our sins upon himself).
Though he was harshly treated, he submitted
And opened not his mouth (he was silent before Herod),
Like a lamb to the slaughter (the Passover Lamb, Lamb of God),
Or a sheep before the shearers (he was stripped naked).

(Isaiah 53:3-7)

David, the Jewish King, speaks in song

"MY GOD, MY GOD, WHY HAVE YOU FORGOTTEN ME?"

This is the first line of a popular Jewish song. Many teenagers recognize it from the popular rock-opera Jesus Christ, Superstar. They will know only the "first" line, but the Jews will know all of the song. It is Psalm 22.

But I am a worm, not a man;
The scorn of men, despised by the people.
All who see me scoff at me;
They mock me with parted lips,
They wag their heads:
"He relied on the Lord;
Let him deliver him,
Let him rescue him, if he loves him." (Psalm 22:7-9)

I am like water poured out;
All my bones are racked.
My heart has become like wax
Melting away within my bosom.
My throat is dried up like baked clay,
My tongue cleaves to my jaws (I'm thirsty!);
Indeed many dogs surround me.
A pack of evildoers closes in upon me;
They have pierced my hands and my feet.
I can count all my bones.
They look on and gloat over me;
They divide my garments among them,
And for my vesture they cast lots. (Psalm 22:15-19)

You Better Believe It!

I believe in God,
    the Father almighty,
Creator of heaven and earth.
And in Jesus Christ, his only Son,
    our Lord;
who was conceived by the Holy Spirit,
born of the Virgin Mary,
suffered under Pontius Pilate,
was crucified, died, and was buried.
He descended into hell;
the third day he arose again from the dead;
he ascended into heaven,
    sits at the right hand of God,
    the Father almighty;
from thence he shall come
    to judge the living and the dead.
I believe in the Holy Spirit,
    the holy Catholic Church,
        the communion of saints,
    the forgiveness of sins,
the resurrection of the body,
and life everlasting.
Amen.

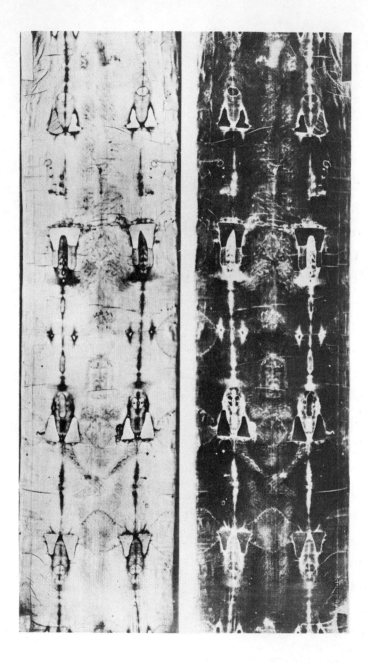

Science Is Against Religion!

If that is true,
It is strange that
Science speaks out
While the Church retains
A cautious silence
About the cloth fourteen feet long,
Allegedly the shroud in which
Jesus was wrapped
For burial.
Science tells us that it
Contains a negative image
Of a crucified man
Whose side was pierced,
Whose head was crowned with thorns,
Whose body was scourged.
It is photographic science
That claims conclusively
That it is truly photographic.
It is artistic science that
Tells us that it is not
A mere painting.
It is medical science that
Gives its infallible evidence
To its corporal authenticity.
And now, the latest evidence is
Supplied by a Swiss criminologist
As to its age.
If this is truly
The photographic impression
Of Jesus on the cloth,
Then how did this image
Get there?

Expert corroborates age of Holy Shroud

TURIN, Italy (NC) — A non-Catholic criminologist specializing in analysis of micro-particles has affirmed that the Holy Shroud of Turin definitely dates back to the time of Christ.

The announcement capped a series of similar reports in recent years indicating that the cloth venerated in Turin's cathedral may indeed be the linen which covered the body of Christ after the Crucifixion.

Max Frei, a 63-year-old criminologist expert from Zurich, Switzerland, declared recently that certain pollen fossils taken from the shroud could only have originated from plants which grew exclusively in Palestine and only in the time of Christ.

Frei, who isolated six such Palestine pollen fossils from the shroud, declared "I don't know if the body of Christ was wrapped in the sheet or if this is the linen mentioned in the Gospel. But I can state with certainty that this cloth dates from the time of Christ."

The Archbishop Speaks

By Archbishop Philip M. Hannan

Little scientific doubt about Turin shroud

...here is probab[ly] more startling [than] resting relic in [Chris]tianity than th[e] Shroud of Turi[n]. According to C[hurch] tradition, it [is the] shroud in which [the] body of Christ was [laid] after his crucifix[ion]. The impression on [the cloth] of a bearded ma[n with] excellent physical pr[opor]tions, about six feet in h[eight.] The person [with] crucifixion or sin[s ...] of execution and [suf]fered a he[avy] flagellation be[fore] death.

For centuries [it was] kept in an elabo[rate ...] years ago, the Turin Fair ma[de ...] controversy ha[s ...]

No one is obliged to believe the shroud preserved today in the Cathedral of Turin was Christ's but a growing body of Catholics hold the covering as sacred, according to Father Roberts.

During his recent tour of Toronto Catholic high schools, Father Roberts, 45, maintained there is little scientific doubt the image on the shroud was created by some miraculous means.

The shroud has somehow been stained in such a way that the body imprint on the cloth was a negative. This, according to scientific research, could only have been caused by an intensely intense flash of light, Father Roberts said.

He maintained the fact of the negative imprint rules out the claim by critics the shroud is an ancient or medieval forgery. No artist could have fabricated details that could only be fully discerned with the help of a 19th century invention — the camera.

The photographs taken of the linen cloth reveal the marks of the likeness of a man who was subjected to a crown of thorns, crucified and whose side was pierced by a lance.

Scientists Say Jesus Was 5-10, 175 Pounds

COLORADO SPRINGS, Colo., Nov. 27 — tists, who have spent the last three years which the body of Christ was believed to was 5-10 and weighed 175 pounds.

Using 45-year-old lantern slides made [of] the Cathedral of Turin, Italy, the two men down on a piece of muslin identical in size on. On that basis, the two researchers, C[...] instructor with a doctorate in aero-mec[hanics] Jackson, an instructor whose doctorate i[s in ...] which were on the shroud to the piece of n[...]

"We did the body outlines in black, w[ith ...] scorch marks in orange and water mark[s ...] "Then we draped the cloth over the [...] aligned with the corresponding part of [...] were lined up to touch the subject, since [...]

No Contradiction to Authenticity Of Christ's Linen Seen in Study

VATICAN CITY (AP) — An exhaustive seven-year investigation of the Holy Shroud of Christ shows it cannot be dismissed as a fake relic, a leader of the study team said Saturday.

But he said the experts recommended more tests on what is truthfully held to be the actual linen cloth wrapped around Christ's body after the crucifixion.

"We have not found anything negative (to contradict the belief)," the Rt. Rev. Jose Cottino, vice president of the commission of experts, said in a telephone interview from the northern city of Turin, where the 14-by-three-foot relic is kept in a silver chest.

While the commission's report will not be definitive, he said, it will at least deny that the tradition of the shroud can be dismissed as a myth.

Msgr. Cottino, a native of New Bedford, Mass., said the final report of the commission, established with Vatican approval, will be made public next week.

He said the experts concluded the cloth "could have come from the area and time of our Lord."

Msgr. Cottino said the chief significance in the panel's findings is that extensive photographic and other tests on the Holy Shroud failed to disprove its authenticity.

Msgr. Cottino said the commission found no definite trace of blood on the cloth. Some students of the Holy Shroud say possible blood stains on it could indicate Christ did not die on the Cross but was still bleeding and died later.

Pope Paul VI suggested five years ago that special studies be conducted on the "Shroud of Turin."

The body was placed in the cloth without washing as evidenced by the blood stains and was removed after several days before corruption set in.

While there is dispute among scholars about the authenticity of the shroud, the harmony between the Gospel account of the Passion of Christ and the sufferings of the man in the shroud are too great to be mere coincidence, Father Roberts said.

Several popes have expressly declared their faith in the relic's genuineness even though the Church takes no official stand on its authenticity.

In 1931, Pope Pius XI said: "We speak now as a scientist and not as Pope. We have made a personal study of the Holy Shroud and are convinced of its authenticity. Objections have been raised but they do not hold water."

Pope Pius XII in 1950 spoke of the shroud as "an extraordinary witness to the passion of our divine Saviour."

And Pope John XXIII was known to be devoted to the shroud. At the time of his death he was reported to be planning a public exposition of the relic.

A Vatican spokesman said the report of the commission had not arrived at the Vatican but will be studied when it reaches the Central administration of the Roman Catholic Church.

The spokesman said he did not know if the Vatican will take a stand on the commission's final report. He said the investigation was left to the competence of the archdiocese of Turin.

The shroud is wrapped in red silk and kept in a silver chest on an altar, protected by a glass cover and iron grills. It contains an impressed face and the shape of the body believed to be Christ's.

The material is the property of Italy's former royal family, the House of Savoy. It is rarely made public — and has been opened no more than 10 times in the last

(Continued on Page 6-A, Col. 5)

...d — aside from the ...m the fifth or sixth ...ak of veneration of the ...ople's imperial palace. ...'s fall to the Turks was

...was only one v[...] who fit it exa[ctly ...] ...xoth 30 years o[...] ...roject. Jackso[n ...] ...a a teen-ager [...] ...of the shroud [...] ...ns: nail mark[s ...] ...a lance wound [...] ...ade by a crow[n ...]

...olese. ...possession of [...] ...d still belong [...] ...of Italy. ...ear docum[...] ...eration of t[...] ...n 1354 ...ST CHRISTI.

What if a brilliant
Light or radiant energy
Exuded from the body
Of Jesus at the
Moment of Resurrection?
Did he not radiate such
Light at the Transfiguration?
What is even stranger
Is that something
That the Church
Does not require us to believe
Brings faith more easily.
But it is not really strange,
For Jesus said,
UNLESS YOU SEE SIGNS AND WONDERS,
YOU WILL NOT BELIEVE.

Power Signs...or Symbols

As an Englishman, the American flag
Was just another flag to me.
I recognized it as a symbol of the
United States.
It gave me no feelings.
It had no power in my life
Until I lived in the United States
And came to know the things
It stood for.
On my return to England for a
Short vacation
I saw that same flag flying
Over the American Embassy
In London.
It immediately gave me a feeling
Of warmth, of homesickness
For the country for which it stood.
I believed in America
So now this sign of America
Had power to move me.
Its power was not in the flag itself
But in me.
A symbol has no power
Unless it is believed in.
For Protestant Christians
The sacraments are such symbols.
Baptism is a symbolic sign
Of the believers' faith in Christ.

It has no power in itself unless
The one being baptized believes in Christ.
It is only a symbolic sign,
So they do not baptize babies,
For babies cannot believe.
The light switch is also a sign.
It is the sign of light.
If I use that sign
The light comes on
Whether I believe it will or not.
The power is in the sign itself.
It is a *power* sign.
Catholics baptize babies because
For us the sacraments are
Power signs.
They are signs that *do* what they *show*.
A radio switch brings the sound of music.
A television button brings a picture.
A turn of a knob and the air is cooled
By the air conditioner.
The same power under a different sign
Can heat the room in winter
Or freeze food in a freezer.
It can dry my hair or
Wash my clothes.
These power signs tell me that
Electricity is present.
The sign makes that power work in my life.
It has nothing to do with my belief in the sign.
For Catholics, the seven sacraments
Are not symbolic signs
Like a flag or
A cross.
They are *Power* signs
Like a light switch.
They are signs of Christ's power.

When they are used
They make
Christ present in my life.
They do what the sign shows.

THE SACRAMENTS ARE STILL "IN"

Baptism turns on the light of Christ. *Confirmation* increases and fortifies that light. *Holy Eucharist* really feeds me with the body and blood of Jesus. *Confession* reconciles me to God and turns the light back on after it has been turned off by sin. *Marriage* welds a couple together in God. *Holy Orders* really gives God-power to priests. And the *Sacrament of the Sick* really heals the soul and, if God so wills, the body too.

For us Catholics, the sacraments are *Power Signs* —not mere symbols like a flag.

The Initiation

Baptism is not merely a symbolic washing,
It really washes clean.
It's as cleansing to the soul
As a shower is to the body.
It is not just a symbolic gesture
By which I say, "Count me in."
It is a *power* sign.
Which gives the life of Jesus,
As water gives life to a seed
Planted in the ground.
It really makes me a brother or a sister
Of Christ and an heir to him in his kingdom.
I am born again as a child of God.
God then is truly my father.
Jesus then is my real brother.
And Mary is my mother too.
Since we share the same spiritual
Parents and the same divine brother,
We are truly
BROTHERS AND SISTERS IN THE LORD.
It is the sacrament by which we are born,
Without which we are incapable of
Receiving fruitfully the other
Sacraments . . . or *Power* signs.

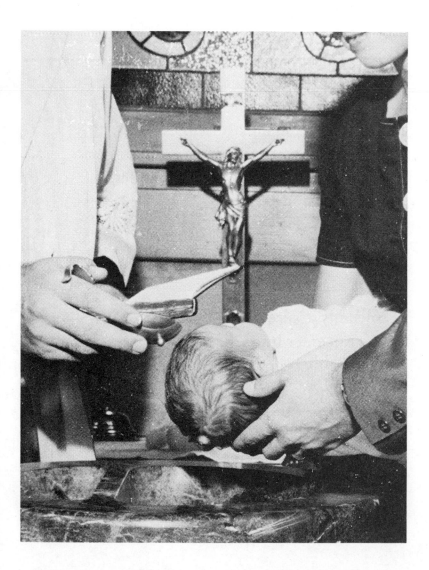

"Full authority has been given to me
both in heaven and on earth;
go, therefore, and make disciples
of all the nations.
Baptize them in the name of the Father,
    and of the Son,
    and of the Holy Spirit."

Matthew 28.18-19

"I solemnly assure you,
no one can enter into God's kingdom
without being begotten of water and Spirit."

John 3.5

"I Never Chose to Be a Christian"

At Baptism, Christ chose you.
In Confirmation, you choose Christ.
At birth you became your parent's child.
As an adult you choose to call them "Mom" and "Dad."
In Confirmation, you become an adult Christian,
You freely choose to call God your father,
And the Spirit confirms this relationship
With oil and the Laying-on of hands.
You receive the same Spirit as Jesus
And the sevenfold gifts to help you live a Christian life.
A chicken's egg is fertilized and has chicken life.
In Baptism you received Christ life.
The egg is hatched and becomes a chicken.
In Confirmation you are hatched and
Become another Christ.
"It is no longer I that live but
Christ who lives in me," says St. Paul.
As oil applied to the body strengthens,
So oil applied to the soul
Strengthens the spiritual muscles.
It's not just a symbolic gesture
But a *Power* sign.

When the apostles in Jerusalem
heard that Samaria had accepted
the word of God,
they sent Peter and John to them.
The two went down to these people
and prayed that they might receive
the Holy Spirit.
It had not as yet come down upon any of them
since they had only been baptized
in the name of the Lord Jesus.

Acts 8.14-16

The pair upon arriving imposed hands on them
and they received the Holy Spirit.

Acts 8.17

Let us, then,
go beyond the initial teaching about Christ
and advance to maturity,
not laying the foundation
all over again:
>   repentance from dead works,
>   faith in God,
>   instruction about baptisms and
>   laying on of hands. . . .

Hebrews 6.1-2

It Looks Like Bread,
It Tastes Like Bread

A young boy about to make his first Communion was questioned by the pastor.

"What will you receive next Sunday?" he was asked.

"Bread and Wine."

"Try again, it's not just bread and wine, is it, Johnny?"

"It is bread and wine! It looks like bread. It tastes like bread and it feels like bread. It is bread! And that wine business—it looks, tastes and smells like wine, and that's what it is. It's wine! So it is bread and wine."

The pastor refused to let Johnny receive the sacrament, so the boy was sent to me.

"What's your problem, Johnny?" I asked.

"I don't have a problem. The priest has the problem. He thinks that bread and wine is Jesus," he said defiantly.

I smiled at the stubbornness of this very intelligent eight-year-old.

"I believe it is Jesus, too, Johnny," I said.

"Then *you* gotta problem too!" was his quick answer.

It is a problem
Understanding Christ's real presence
Under the appearance of
Bread and Wine.
It's a mystery!

Electricity is truly present
In the radio,
The refrigerator,
The television,
The lightbulb,
And the air conditioner.
The things it touches have not changed,
But the power is contained within those things.
Yet we can see them working,
At least see the effects of electricity's presence.
How about radiation?
If I exposed bread and wine to
Radiation,
the bread would still taste like bread,
Look like bread,
Feel like bread.
The wine would still taste like wine,
Look like wine,
Smell like wine.
But I'd better not eat or drink them—
I would become *radioactive!*
It would be radioactive power
Under the appearance of bread and wine
And none of my senses could tell me that.
BUT YOU BETTER BELIEVE IT!

It's the Real Thing!

For Catholics, the Eucharist
Is not just a symbol or
A sign, like a flag.
It is a *Power* sign.
It is Christ himself.
Some Christians can't accept this.
They won't let Jesus love them that much.
But what if he really does love you
That much?
Do you think that is harder
Than becoming man? Too hard for God?
If God can't do that, how do you think
He could become a man?
If a teenage girl had a chance to date
Her TV idol,
To go out with him, to dine with him,
To dance with him, to kiss him—or
to have his voice on a tape recorder
To listen to and his picture to look at,
Which would she want?
YOU BETTER BELIEVE IT—THE REAL THING!
So why would a Christian people prefer a symbol
To the REAL THING!

During the meal,
Jesus took the bread,
  blessed it,
  broke it,
and gave it to his disciples.
"Take this and eat it," he said,
"this is my body."

Then he took a cup,
  gave thanks,
and gave it to them.
"All of you must drink from it," he said,
"for this is my blood,
the blood of the covenant,
to be poured out in behalf of many
for the forgiveness of sins."

Matthew 26.26-28

Proof of Love

At Johnny's first Communion, I asked him whom he loved most in all the world. "My dog!" he replied.

"How much do you love your dog? Could you show me?"

Johnny stretched out his arms in the shape of a cross. "That much."

I asked him to look at Jesus on the large crucifix behind the altar. Jesus had his arms outstretched too.

"Do you love your dog *that* much, Johnny?" I pointed to the crucifix.

Johnny looked up at Jesus above his head and nodded, his arms still outstretched.

"If you really do love your dog that much, I can tell you how to prove it. Why don't you give up that party after Mass, the hamburgers and the hot dogs and the ice cream. Give up your nice clean bed, your friends, your football. Give up being a little boy. I'll wave a magic wand and you can become a dog! You can live in a kennel and eat bones and dog biscuits."

Johnny shook his head, "No! I don't love him that much!" Johnny lowered his arms.

"But Jesus loves you that much. He loves you enough to become a boy, to talk like a boy, to eat like a boy, to play like a boy—and to die like a man. 'Greater love has no man than to lay down his life for his friend.' That cross is the greatest sign of Jesus' love for you as a man. But Jesus is also God, and he can show even greater love than that. If a boy doesn't love his dog enough to become a dog, he certainly doesn't love him enough to become a dog biscuit. The greatest sign of God's love for us as God is Jesus, *who becomes our food.*"

Who Needs Confession?

Confession is out of favor among young people.
In high schools in city after city,
Kids are turned off by it.
Ninety per cent of our youth have ceased to go.
It's true, but a negative truth!
The positive truth is that 10 per cent still go.
When asked why they do not go to Confession,
They answer, "I don't believe in it. . . .
I don't need a priest to have my sins forgiven."
True. They don't need a priest
To have their sins forgiven,
For Christ has forgiven every sin
By his death on the cross, *but*
The sacrament of reconciliation
Takes away sin, and then there is
Nothing to forgive.
Supposing a man commits adultery.
His wife may forgive him,
But he still is an adulterer,
A *forgiven* adulterer.
A teenager steals from a store.
The manager forgives him,
But he is still a thief,
A *forgiven* thief.
A young girl lies to her mother.
Though the mother forgives her,
The child is still a liar,
A *forgiven* liar.

If those sins could be taken away,
Then the adulterer would no longer
Be an adulterer.
The thief no longer a thief
And the liar no longer a liar.
Christ gave that power to his apostles
When he breathed on them and gave them
The Holy Spirit.
A priest doesn't merely forgive sins,
He takes them away in Jesus' name.
It is not just a symbolic gesture—
It is a *power* sign.
Sin is *really* removed, and man
Is reconciled to God and the Church.
Every Christian, Catholic or Protestant,
Believes that Baptism washes away sin.
Every Christian, Catholic or Protestant,
Believes in the necessity of Baptism.
You can't say to a Protestant minister,
"I believe in Jesus but I don't believe in
Your power to baptize me."
Baptists, Presbyterians, Methodists, and
Evangelicals won't accept you into their
Community without Baptism.
So what about the sins after Baptism?
Is it logical to believe that one
Ceremonial sign can take away sin
And another can't?
The Catholic Church teaches that
My deliberate rejection of God's commands,
With full knowledge,
Kills the life of Jesus in me and
Cuts me off from the family
Of the Church.
Just as I was born into
That family through Baptism,

So I am restored to that family
Through reconciliation,
A sacrament that is no less a *power* sign
Than Baptism.
What would you sooner be?
A forgiven sinner,
Or one whose sins have been taken away?
Someone who has been restored to innocence!
It was the immense love of Jesus
That gave us this sacrament of
Peace, a peace the world cannot give.
A priest can very often do in minutes
What takes a psychiatrist years.
If only we would all believe that.
On retreats, I get 90 per cent of the kids
To go to Confession
By offering to *take away*
Their sins,
Not just to "forgive" them.

Then he breathed on them and said:
"Receive the Holy Spirit.
If you forgive men's sins,
    they are forgiven them.
If you hold them bound,
    they are bound."

John 20.22-23

When Jesus saw their faith,
he said to the paralyzed man,
"My son, your sins are forgiven."

Now some of the scribes were sitting
there asking themselves:
"Why does the man talk in that way?
He commits blasphemy!
Who can forgive sins
    except God alone?"

*[They said it about Jesus before they
        said it about his priests.]*

Jesus was immediately aware of their reasoning,
though they kept it to themselves, and he
said to them: ". . . That you may know
the Son of Man has authority on earth
to forgive sins, I command [this paralyzed man]:
Stand up! Pick up your mat and go home."

                                            Mark 2.5-11

A Priest

If asked to indicate the two things
That turn kids off the most,
I would answer:
The Mass, "It's boring."
And Confession. "I don't believe in it."
Perhaps it is diabolical?
The two things that kids like the least
Are the only two things
That are strictly priestly.
Destroy faith in the Mass,
Destroy faith in Confession,
And you destroy the Catholic priesthood.
Destroy the priesthood and
You destroy the Catholic Church.

A Baptist minister who introduced me on
A Baptist radio program
Suggested that being a priest and
Being a minister were the same thing.
It was just a question of terminology.
"Aren't we both the same, Reverend?"
He asked.
I answered his question by asking him one.

"What do you claim you can do that
An ordinary Christian does not have the
Power to do?"
"Why, nothing. I have no additional power
Above any other Christian."
"Well, then there is a difference between us.
Priests claim they have the power
To change bread and wine into the
Body and Blood of Jesus and
To take away sins.
If these claims are true—and if we are
Claiming more than you—there is an
Enormous difference between us."
The minister conceded that.

A priest does not take this office on himself.
He must be chosen by one who has
The power to ordain (the bishop).
Putting a Roman collar around your neck
Doesn't make you a priest.
Merely wanting to preach and have a church
Doesn't make you a priest.
Christ chose his apostles.
The apostles chose their successors.
Let's use the analogy of electricity.
If you are touching something that has a
Live electric current running through it,
The power goes through you too.
If you touch me, the power passes to me.
If I touch another, the power passes to him.
And so it continues, as long as the link
Is maintained.
This is what the Church means by *Apostolic succession*. The power comes through Jesus to the apostles, to the bishops and priests today.

Follow Me

Jesus calls men to follow him *now*,
Just as he did in the Bible.
He is still calling men,
But men are often deaf to his call,
Like the rich man who asked him,
"What must I do to possess eternal life?"
When Jesus led him step by step,
He listened until that final step:
"Leave everything and follow me."
He was a rich young man.
To leave everything was an obstacle.
Today, young men have so many
Exciting and interesting things to do.
"I want to be a football player, a doctor,
A lawyer, a pilot, a writer, a senator,
A psychiatrist, or . . . a traveler."

The priesthood seems dull by comparison,
Doesn't it?
Until, that is, you realize that whereas a priest can do *any*thing
Any man can do,
Only a priest can do what a priest
Can do.
Priests are lawyers, doctors, pilots,
Writers, senators, travelers, and even football players.
WHAT CAN BE MORE EXCITING THAN JESUS
CALLING YOU AND CHOOSING YOU TO BE
AN EXTENSION OF HIMSELF?
To be his hands at Mass.
To be his ears and mouth in the

Sacrament of reconciliation.
What can be more exciting than
Feeding the spiritually hungry
With the Body of Christ or
Taking away the sins of the world?
What if he is calling *you*?
What stands in your way?
Will you make the final step
If you hear,
      "COME, FOLLOW ME"?

At that they nominated two,
Joseph . . . and Matthias.
Then they prayed:
"O Lord, you read the hearts of men.
Make known to us
which of these you choose
for this apostolic ministry,
replacing Judas. . . ."

Then they drew lots between the two men.
The choice fell to Matthias,
who was added to the eleven apostles. . . .

In each church
they ordained prebyters [priests].

Acts 1.23-26, 14.23

Why Not Live Together?

Who needs that piece of paper?
Why not just move in together?
It's becoming more and more
The popular thing to do.
Movie stars and celebrities lead the way,
And it is easy to follow their example.
A television hero announces it publicly
During a talk show.
A college student states it
Privately to shocked parents.
"We love each other, and that piece of
Paper doesn't mean a thing."
Yet, thousands of young people continue
To come to churches and demand their
Right to walk down the aisle—
The bride in her white gown, accompanied by
Her bridesmaids in pastel shades,
The groom waiting nervously in
Flamboyant tuxedo with his friends, who
Feel awkward, missing their jeans.
They pull their cuffs and straighten their
Ties, and they cough.
The candles are lit, the organ plays.
  I do.
  I do.
The priest's questions are answered,
And the rings are exchanged.
But . . . "I do" *what?*
If a wedding is just a pretty ritual,

An opportunity to get dressed up
Prior to getting undressed,
If it is merely society's permission
To sleep together,
Then FORGET IT!
That piece of paper doesn't mean a thing.
Christian marriage is between a boy and a girl
Who wish to proclaim their love for each other
Publicly and intend that they make a covenant
Between the two of them and God.
They make public vows before witnesses
In the presence of God—to remain
True to each other, excluding all others,
To love and to cherish each other
In good times and bad.
For richer, for poorer,
In sickness and in health.
Till death.
It is a permanent union,
Not a symbolic gesture.
A *power* sign in which
God welds them to each other
and to himself.
It is not a civil union granted by a
Piece of paper.
It is a Christian marriage of two
Joined by God,
From whom new life may come.
A PERFECT MARRIAGE IS A PERFECT TRIANGLE.

"For this reason
a man shall leave his mother and father
and shall cling to his wife,
and the two shall be made into one.
This is a great foreshadowing;
I mean that it refers to Christ as the church.
In any case,
each one should love his wife
as he loves himself,
the wife for her part
showing respect for her husband.

Ephesians 5.31-33

To those now married, however,
I give this command
(though it is not mine;
it is the Lord's):
A wife must not separate from her husband.
If she does separate,
she must either remain single
or become reconciled to him again.
Similarly,
a husband must not divorce his wife.

1 Corinthians 7.10-11

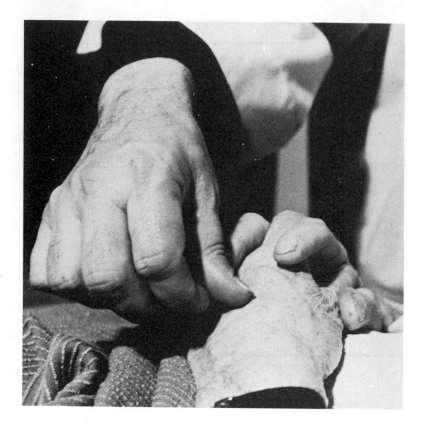

A Healing Touch

Until Vatican II,
This sacrament, or *power sign,*
Was called Extreme Unction, but
Mostly it was referred to as
The Last Rites.
The name has been changed to
Stress its original purpose.
It is a *healing* sacrament,
Not just a rite to prepare a man
For death.
It is a *powerful* healing touch
That removes all sin.
And very often it restores physical health.
It is not a symbolic gesture,
It is a real *power* sign.
The Church wishes more people
Would take advantage of this sacrament,
So the name has been changed.
It is now called
The Sacrament of the Sick.

Is there anyone sick among you? Let him bring in the priests of the Church and let them pray over him, anointing him with oil in the name of the Lord, and the prayer of faith will save the sick man . . . and if he be in sins, they shall be forgiven him.

James 5.14

"Why Catholic?"

What makes a car a car?
Wheels, steering column, brakes,
Engine, seats,
All contained in the body.
All cars have them in common.
But what makes one car a Cadillac
And another a Volkswagen?
Things they do not have in common,
Things that make them different.

Our common belief in Jesus
Makes us Christian.
The beliefs we do not share
Make us uniquely different.
They let us say
"I am a Catholic Christian,
A Roman Catholic."

When Cadillac advertises,
It sells its cars not by
Reminding us what makes it a car
But what makes it a Cadillac.
Power Brakes, Power Steering, Power Seats,
Power Windows, Stereo and Cruise Control
Are optional with other cars,
But with Cadillac, they're standard!
They come with the car.
Catholics have everything that

Other Christians have *but also*
The seven sacraments, the Mass,
Christ's real presence in the Eucharist and
Mary as our Mother—all optional with
Other Christians.
With us, they're standard.
THEY COME WITH THE CHURCH!

Sometimes you may see a car
That looks like a Cadillac
Because its owner has put a
Cadillac body on it.
But that doesn't make it a Cadillac.
Some Catholics may be hiding under
A Catholic appearance, but
Unless you believe *all* that the
Catholic Church teaches
You are not a real Catholic!

> *The seven sacraments, the Mass, the Real Presence,*
> *A teaching Church and our mother Mary are not*
> *options*
> *That I can take or leave. They are*
> *Standard.*
> *To drop them means to cease to be Catholic.*

Some other Christians who have taken
These same options call themselves

Catholics too—
Orthodox, Anglicans, Episcopalians.
Those who reject some
Or all of these options
Are called
Protestants.

"But Christians Are Divided . . ."

Christians are divided
Because man is divided.
Aren't good people divided over
Politics, music, dress, language?
As long as man is man
He will continue to be divided
Unless God himself makes man one.

As Roman Catholics, we believe that
God gave us a rock of unity.
That rock is Peter,
To whom Christ gave the
KEYS TO THE KINGDOM,
The power to bind and to loose on earth.
This one teaching alone separates the world's
Largest religion, six hundred million Roman Catholics,
From the next largest group of Christians,
The Eastern Orthodox. They, too, recognize the Pope
As the successor of St. Peter,
But only as the "first among equals,"
Not as a supreme shepherd.

"The Pope Is Just a Man"

Abraham was chosen by God.
>*He was just a man.*
Isaac was the shepherd of the flock.
>*He was just a man.*
Jacob inherited his father's role.
>*He was just a man.*
Joseph was the recognized spokesman
For God's people.
>*He was just a man.*
Moses certainly spoke with and for God.
>*He was just a man.*
King David, the model of Israel, sinned.
>*He was just a man.*
Isaiah told the people unpopular truths.
>*He was just a man.*
Jeremiah would not have won a primary,
Though he spoke with God's voice.
>*He was just a man.*
In every age, one man has spoken under
God's guidance.
The majority of God's people did not listen.

Simon becomes Peter.
>*He was just a man.*
Peter, the rock, is given the
Keys of the Kingdom.
>*He was just a man.*

Peter can bind and loose
Upon earth.
He was just a man.
Peter is the shepherd of the
Whole flock.
He was just a man.
John XXIII calls the Vatican Council.
He was just a man.
John XXIII is loved by all.
He was just a man.
Paul VI, the 263rd successor to
Peter, was not so popular.
He was just a man. . . .

"Why a Pope?"

Throughout the Bible,
There is always one man
Who speaks with God's voice,
A *sign of unity.*
It does not depend upon a popular vote.
The popular vote went against Moses in the desert.
The people made a golden calf and worshiped it.
They complained and rebelled against Moses
And his teachings.

According to surveys and polls,
Sixty per cent of Catholics in the United States
No longer listen to the Pope.
They rebel.
They make a golden calf of materialism.
They worship at the altar of luxury and pleasure.
They consider the Pope irrelevant in the twentieth century.

The people of God were bored in the desert.
They wanted more exciting worship.
Moses prayed alone on a mountaintop.
His people celebrated according to the ways of the world.
But Moses was still God's voice for them.
And his teaching was that of God.
Pope John Paul II is the successor of St. Peter.
He is considered outdated,
Irrelevant, and not "with it."
As he prays on Vatican Hill alone,

He alone remains the sole successor
To a man named Peter.
THE ROCK OF UNITY!
No other Church makes such
A claim,
And history traces an
Unbroken line of names
From Peter, the apostle of Rome,
To John Paul II, the Bishop of Rome.
I am a Catholic
Not because the pope *may* speak infallibly.
It is enough for me,
As it was for the
Fathers of the Church
And for centuries of saints,
To belong to a Church
That claims Peter's successor.
FOR WHERE MOSES WAS,
THERE TOO WAS THE PEOPLE OF GOD.
WHERE PETER IS,
THERE IS THE CHURCH OF JESUS.

"He who hears you, hears me.
He who rejects you, rejects me."

". . . who do you say that I am?"
"You are the Messiah," Simon Peter answered,
"the Son of the living God."
Jesus replied, "Blest are you,
Simon son of Jonah!
No mere man has revealed this to you,
but my heavenly Father.
I . . . declare to you,
you are 'Rock,'
and on this rock I will build my church,
and the jaws of death shall not prevail against it.
I will entrust to you
the keys of the kingdom of heaven.
Whatever you declare bound on earth
shall be bound in heaven;
whatever you declare loosed on earth
shall be loosed in heaven."

Matthew 16.15-19

Jesus the Good Shepherd
hands over the flock to Peter:

When they had eaten their meal,
Jesus said to Simon Peter,
"Simon, son of John,
do you love me more than these?"
"Yes, Lord," he said,
"You know that I love you."
At which Jesus said, "Feed my lambs."
    A second time he put his question,
"Simon, son of John, do you love me?"
"Yes, Lord," Peter said,
"you know that I love you."
Jesus replied, "Tend my sheep."
    A third time Jesus asked him. . . .
Peter . . . said to him, "Lord,
you know everything.
You know well that I love you."
Jesus said to him, "Feed my sheep."

John 21.15-17

Why
All the Costumes,
Candles,
Statues and Stuff?

All this is another way of saying
RITUAL.
Those who criticize the Church
For all its rituals
Have their birthday cakes,
The candles,
The "Happy Birthday" song.
Friends gather for the party.
Isn't this ritual?
Even Godless countries
Have a national anthem,
A flag to be raised,
National days of celebration,
Parades and marching bands.
Isn't this ritual?
Fraternities and sororities
Have their initiation rites,
Ceremonies, and songs
Unique to their group.
Isn't this ritual?
There are Valentine cards with flowery verses.
There are masked faces of children on Halloween.
Hands cross their hearts as the
Stars and Stripes is raised. There flies
Old Glory, waving proudly in the breeze
On Independence Day—and
Isn't this ritual?
The anti-establishment radicals

Once raised clenched fists.
Silent protestors march for
Whatever cause is important to them.
Groups of apathetic kids
Seek a "high" by
Passing the same "joint"
From mouth to mouth.
Isn't this ritual?
There are Christmas trees,
Mistletoe, holly wreaths,
Brightly colored lights.
Confetti on New Year's Eve.
And, of course, a kiss to
"Wish the New Year in."
Isn't this ritual?

God doesn't need all that ritual.
***Man* does!**

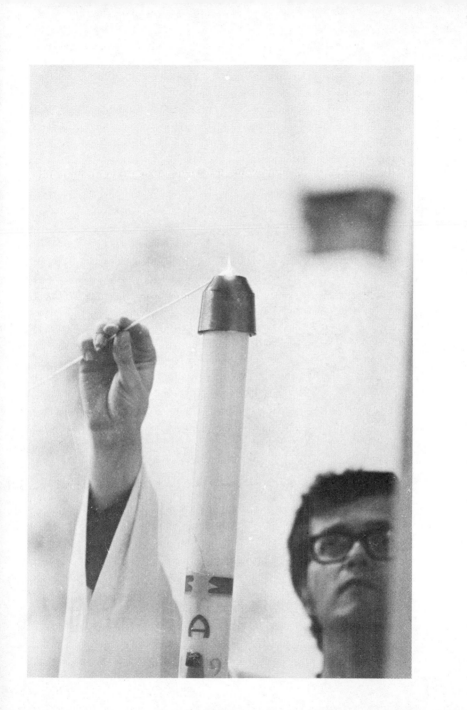

"The Same Old Thing!"

When I first came to this country
Ten years ago, I watched a football game
On television and I had no idea of
What was going on.
Why the weird clothes, padding, helmets?
Why did they get into those little circles?
Why did they keep knocking each other down—
Even the ones who weren't carrying the ball?
What was a "first and ten"?
What was a quarterback?
Everyone was standing, cheering.
"It's a touchdown!"
That I understood. But what was a field goal?
A punt?
An extra point?
I didn't have the vaguest idea.
One Sunday, there were two
Consecutive games on TV,
Six hours of it!
The other priests were glued
To the television, sitting on the
Edges of their chairs,
Munching popcorn.
Suddenly, they would stand, throw their
Arms in the air and yell.
Why? I didn't know. I WAS BORED!

Teenagers would ask,
"Did you see that game yesterday, Father?"
I would nod. "Yes."
"What do you think of our football?"
They would ask proudly.
"It's the same old thing!"
They looked at me in disbelief.
"Then you don't understand the game."
But these same teenagers would say the same
Thing about the Mass.
Mass is the same old thing—it's boring!

When I claimed football was the same
Old thing and boring, I wasn't telling
You a thing about football, but I was
Telling you a lot about me.
When teenagers say that Mass is the
Same old thing and it's boring, they
Aren't telling me a thing about the
Mass, but they are telling me a lot
About themselves.
They don't understand the Mass!
Saying something is
THE SAME OLD THING
Is saying nothing.
Teenage music is the
Same old thing to adults.
Teenage phone calls are the
Same old thing to parents.
Everything we do repeatedly can be
The same old thing.
Eating breakfast, hot dogs, hamburgers;
Going to school, to the movies, on dates;
Sleeping, waking, washing, dressing—
It's the same old thing.
What makes it exciting is not that

It is different and new but
That it is understood and we can
Relate ourselves to it.
Mass is the same very old thing.
Millions of people have been very
Excited about it for two thousand years.
Excited enough to walk miles to get to it.
Excited enough to go daily.
Excited enough to die for it.
WHY?
They understood what it was all about.

"I Don't Get Anything Out of It"

"When was the last time God spoke to you?"
Every time I ask kids that question
They give me a weird look
And wonder about me.
If you went to Mass last Sunday,
God definitely spoke to you
During the readings and the homily.
So, what was it about?
You can't remember?
That's serious, for it was God's Word
That was read to you.
Not only to you but
To the whole world.
It was read in English, French, German,
Chinese, Italian, Spanish, Polish—
In every language,
Wherever there is a
Catholic church.
It was not a private reading
But a public proclamation
Of God's Word to the whole Church.
It was for the Pope, bishops, priests,
Parents and children,
In every country, city and village,
Those same readings read in
Your parish church.
Liturgy of the Word
Means the public reading for

The whole Church.
God did speak to you?
What did he say?

One time, on a college campus,
After the readings
I didn't preach,
But I did say,
"I'm giving away record albums
After Mass in the sacristy."
What a crowd gathered at the door!
"Where are the albums, Father?"
They asked.
"Did you hear me say that?
Now tell me, what did Jesus say?"
The looked puzzled and couldn't answer.
That day Christ was giving them
Eternal Life.
They didn't hear that
But they did hear me say
That I was giving away records.

My word will not come back to me empty, says the Lord.

Isaiah 55.11

When the Mass was outlawed in my own
Country, England, by Elizabeth I,
Hundreds of young Englishmen
Left their homeland,
Studied for the priesthood and
Returned to England and certain death
Because they would celebrate a Mass.
Loyal Catholics, including teenagers,
Risked their lives to attend these

Secret Masses.
WHY?
Because they understood them.
Mother Teresa of Calcutta,
Who works so hard among the poor,
The dying and the destitute, says,
"Without daily Mass, I could not do
This work for more than a week."
WHY?
Because she understands it.
I know teenagers who go to Mass every day.
WHY?
Because they know why the priest is
Wearing those "vestments."
They know what the liturgy of the Word means.
They know what is happening when the
Priest raises the host and chalice.
They know why they walk up the aisle
To receive Holy Communion.
IT IS THE CENTER OF THEIR CATHOLIC LIFE!

Let's Make a Deal

In the Old Testament, the Jews
Offered a sacrifice.
Each family bought a lamb at Passover.
It was slain by the priest, and the blood
Of the lamb was sprinkled on those present to
Remind them that the lamb died for their sins.
It was God's way of "making a deal" with them,
And they with God. They took this lamb
Home afterward and ate it during a holy meal.
This deal was called a covenant.
"I will be your God, and you will be my people."
They called this lamb the *Lamb of God*.
John the Baptist called Jesus that too.
"Look, there is the Lamb of God Who takes away
The sins of the world."
Jesus is the lamb of the New Testament who was
Slain at Passover for our sins,
Whose body we eat in a Holy Meal. Each time
We do it, God makes a deal with us, and we with him.
We are present at Calvary as Jesus dies.
We are present at the Resurrection.
Not that Christ is doing it all over again.
When you see a repeat of a television movie,
The actors are not "doing it" all over again.
But we *are* present at the "original."
Through the priest we are present
At the original sacrifice, and
Each time the sacrifice is offered,
The covenant is renewed.

God makes a deal with us
as we complete our part of the deal
in Holy Communion.

How can this be boring?

Eucharist means "thanks."
So "liturgy of the Eucharist"
means public thanksgiving to our God
as we renew the covenant.

Every time, then, you eat this bread
and drink this cup,
you proclaim the death of the Lord
until he comes!

1 Corinthians 11.26

Let It Be!

Quite a few years back, the Beatles made a record
Called "Let It Be."
That is the meaning of the word "Amen."
Amen—*Let it be.*
When God says, "Amen," it is.
God says "Amen" to light, and there is light.
God says "Amen" to life, and there is life.
God's "Amen" makes it happen.
During the Mass we have God's "Amen" too.
This is my body. This is my blood.
God's "Amen" makes it happen. Man's "Amen" accepts it.
Let it be for "it is."
Mary said "Amen" to the angel.
Her "Amen" was an acceptance of God's "Amen."
"Let it be done unto me."
Jesus said "Amen" in the garden.
His "Amen" was an acceptance of his Father's will.
"Not my will but yours be done."
For the people of God, the most important prayer
At Mass is the Great Amen.
The priest as God's instrument has uttered God's Amen,
The words of the Consecration, when
Bread and wine became Body and Blood.
At the close of the Eucharistic Prayer, the priest holds up Christ.

Through him,
with him,
in him,
in the unity of the Holy Spirit,
all glory and honor is yours,
almighty Father,
for ever and ever.
Amen.

Let It Be!

For Me!

"Why Do We Have to Go Every Week?"

How would a young man feel if,
After he took his girlfriend home from a date,
She said to him,
"Do I have to see you every week"?
I think he might reply,
"You don't *have* to see me ever!"
He would know too that she didn't much care for him.
When a young person says, "Do I have to go to Mass?"
I think he doesn't much care about God.
You don't *have* to do anything, even for the Lord.
That's why he gave you a free will.
A young man and woman in love
Can't wait to meet each other again.
That's why those who really understand the Mass,
Who believe that God speaks to them there,
Who believe he really is present in the Eucharist,
Who believe he renews the Covenant there,
Who believe that they are present at Calvary again,
Who witness his Resurrection there,
Can't wait to get to Mass.
That's why Mother Teresa of Calcutta and
Convinced Catholics like her attend Mass
Every chance they get.

"When can I see and be with you again, Jesus?"

Tomorrow!

164

"Why Do We Need Mary?"

If you could choose your mother,
What kind of woman
Would she be?
Wouldn't you pick the most perfect
Woman you could find?
Well, God didn't just pick
Any woman.
He picked a perfect woman,
A woman without sin.
A woman who constantly did his will.
If your knowledge of Jesus
Made you grow as a person,
What about Mary's knowledge of Jesus?
Did anybody know Jesus as well
As she did?
She knew the sound of his voice,
The color of his eyes,
His favorite food,
His deepest thoughts and moods.
She lived closely with him
For thirty years.
For her, he worked his first miracle
Even before his time for miracles.
She was at the foot of the cross.
She was present with the apostles,
Praying with them and for them,
When the Holy Spirit came upon them.
Since the earliest times in the Church,

Christians have held her in special honor.
Today the Eastern Orthodox honor her
Even more than do Roman Catholics.
If God is our father
And Jesus is our brother,
Then we share a common mother.
Protestant Christians remind us,
"There is only one mediator with the Father,
And that is the Son."
That is true. Mary is not a mediator
With the Father, but with her Son.
We believe that Mary can pray
With us and for us.
Is there any Catholic or Protestant
Who has not asked another Christian
To pray for him?
Don't Protestant Christians pray for the sick?
Don't Pentecostals pray with and for you?
Then surely it is not inconsistent that Mary,
The first Christian, the archetype of all Christians,
Can do as much for us.

When I go to Mary, I have a prayer group of two.
She and I, together, praying to her Son, Jesus.

At a certain point the wine ran out,
and Jesus' mother told him,
"They have no more wine."

John 2.3

Mirror of Justice
Seat of Wisdom
Mystical Rose
Tower of David
House of Gold
Gate of Heaven
Morning Star
Queen of Angels
Queen of Patriarchs
Queen of . . .

"Why So Many Titles?"

In Europe, a title, not money, is *the* status symbol.
A man doesn't need money if he is a Duke
Or a Prince, a Count or an Earl.
There, when a country wishes to honor a man,
It gives him a title.
Peasants are nobodies in Europe,
Even rich ones.
Pope John XXIII, who was a very poor peasant,
Was asked by a Cardinal,
"Do you intend to give your brother and sister
A title before the coronation, Your Holiness?"
Pope John's eyes twinkled and a big smile
Spread across his face.
"Of course. I intend to give them the greatest
Title a Pope can bestow upon them."
Was he going to make them a prince and a princess?
His smile grew even larger as he put his arm around
The nervous Cardinal.
"The title I bestow upon them is
Brother and sister of the Pope!"
In two thousand years,
The European-dominated Church has bestowed
Many titles on Mary.
But her greatest title
      She received from God—*Mary Mother of God*

"Blessed are you among all women,
and blessed is the fruit of your womb."

Luke 1.42

My Mother, Too?

One evening, walking through the convent grounds,
I passed one of our Good Shepherd girls.
I stopped, surprised.
Here was this sixteen-year-old,
Sent to us by the court as a problem girl.
She certainly didn't look the part.
She was praying as she walked.
She was praying the rosary!
What is even more surprising is that
She wasn't Catholic.
"Cindy, I thought you were a Baptist?"
"I am, Father," she replied, as she continued
To finger the beads.
"And you're saying the rosary?"
Her answer took me off guard,
But it was a wonderful truth:
"She's *my* mother, too, Father!"

For too long, many have thought,
And thought wrongly, that the Bible
Was Protestant and Mary was Catholic.
Well, the Protestants have reminded us
By their valuable witness
That the Bible is Catholic too.
Let us remind them by our love for Mary
That Mary is their mother too!

My being proclaims
the greatness of the Lord;
my spirit finds joy
in God my savior,
for he has looked upon his servant
in her lowliness;
all ages to come
shall call me blessed.

God who is mighty
has done great things for me,
holy is his name.

His mercy is from age to age
on those who fear him.

He has shown might with his arm;
he has confused the proud
in their inmost thoughts.

He has deposed the mighty
from their thrones
and raised the lowly
to high places.

The hungry he has given
every good thing,
while the rich he has sent
empty away.
He has upheld Israel his servant,
ever mindful of his mercy;

Even as he promised our fathers,
promised Abraham
and his descendants
forever.

The Racing Stripe

What makes a car a car?
They all share some qualities.
What makes a Cadillac a Cadillac
Is what makes it *different*.
We have studied what we share as Christians
And what makes us different as Catholics,
But what about those things that make
Us different but have nothing to do with truth?
Things that really don't have anything to do with
Being a Christian or serving God.
Things like making the Sign of the Cross
Before we pray,
Genuflecting before the Blessed Sacrament,
Votive candles before pictures and statues?
They don't really do a thing, do they?

They are like the racing stripe.
It doesn't make the car run any better,
But it gives it class, distinction.
These little things are dying out among the young,
And that's a pity, because they are our racing stripes!
They give us distinction.
When one saw people bless themselves with the
Sign of the Cross or genuflect in church,
One knew they were Catholic.
These practices do not make you a better Christian,
But they give you a distinction and a sense of
Pride in your Catholic heritage.

Why Should I Pray?

Parents know when their child wants an
Ice cream by his drooling,
But they will still expect the child to say, "Please."
Then expect a "Thank you."
So does God.
We pray to say, "Please, God."
We pray to say, "Thank you, God."
We also pray to communicate with God,
To tell him what is on our minds
And to learn what is on his.
We pray so we may grow in the
Knowledge of God, and in our knowledge
Of ourselves.

But the most important reason to pray
Is the reason why we were created,
TO PRAISE GOD AND TO GLORIFY HIM.

When did you pray last!

What about T. M.?

Who needs a guru to learn some magic word
To repeat and repeat in order to pray?
We have *Christian* transcendental meditation.

Just sit upright in a chair,
Both feet flat on the ground,
Hands resting on your knees.
Close your eyes
And breathe in and out very slowly.
Count from ten down to zero
As you breathe in and out,
Letting your mind and body relax
As you do.
Now, as you breathe out, say,
JESUS,
And as you breathe in, say,
FATHER.
Continue to do this for as long as
You need, until you feel the
Presence of God.
This kind of prayer is as old as the Church—
And it is *trinitarian*.
The Spirit that is within you prays
To the Father in the name of Jesus
And gives perfect glory to God.

"What Is Contemplation?"

In life,
We talk, we think, we feel.
So too in prayer.
We begin to pray by talking.
As we grow in prayer, we become more expert,
And we begin to think.
When we think about God and his mysteries,
We are meditating.
Then as we grow still more in the life of prayer,
We *feel!*
When we feel, we are *contemplating.*
Many people, who talk about saying
The rosary, say that it is quite boring
To repeat over and over the same prayer.
But the rosary was meant to be *thought* about.
It should be at least a meditation.
The most exciting way to use the rosary
Is to *feel* the mysteries,
To *contemplate* them.
Even a contemplative can't contemplate
All the time, but
Everybody can contemplate at some time.

Why not try to contemplate the rosary?

The Rosary

The Joyful Mysteries — the feelings of Mary
>   *The Annunciation*
>   *The Visitation*
>   *The Birth of Jesus*
>   *The Presentation of Jesus*
>   *The Finding of Jesus in the Temple*

"How do you feel, Mary?"

The Sorrowful Mysteries — the feelings of Jesus
>   *The Agony in the Garden*
>   *The Scourging*
>   *The Crowning with Thorns*
>   *The Carrying of the Cross*
>   *The Crucifixion*

"How do you feel, Jesus?"

The Glorious Mysteries — the feelings of the early Christians
>   *The Resurrection*
>   *The Ascension*
>   *The Coming of the Holy Spirit*
>   *The Assumption of Mary into Heaven*
>   *The Crowning of Mary as Queen*

"How do you feel, first Christians?"

In each Mystery, you say one Our Father, ten Hail Marys, and
one Glory Be to the Father.

Jesus Has Favorites

"Blessed are the poor in spirit,
  for theirs is the kingdom of heaven.

Blessed are the meek,
  for they shall possess the earth.

*Blessed are they who mourn,
for they shall be comforted.*

Blessed are they who hunger
and thirst for justice,
for they shall be satisfied.

Blessed are the merciful,
for they shall obtain mercy.

Blessed are the clean of heart,
for they shall see God.

Blessed are the peacemakers,
for they shall be called
children of God.

Blessed are they who
   suffer persecution for justice sake,
   for theirs is the kingdom of heaven.

Blessed are you when men reproach you
   and persecute you
   and speak falsely,
   saying all manner of evil against you
   for my sake.

Rejoice and exult,
because your reward
is great in heaven.

For so did they persecute
the prophets
who were before you."

Jesus' Farewell

"As the Father has loved me,
so I have loved you.
Live on in my love.

You will live in my love
if you keep my commandments,
even as I have kept my Father's commandments
and live in his love.

All this I tell you
that my joy may be yours
and your joy may be complete.

This is my commandment:
*Love one another
as I have loved you.*"

John 15.9-12

Pleased?

We hope you found this book to be both informative and interesting. If so, you may wish to know more about the other Religious Books OSV publishes.

Write for our free catalog: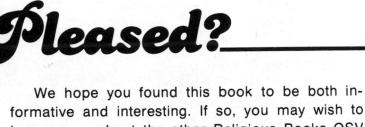

Marketing Department
Religious Books
200 Noll Plaza
Huntington, IN 46750